pg 13 + 14

PG 22 + 23

pg 24

ESP

ESP
The Search
beyond the Senses

Daniel Cohen

Illustrated with photographs

HARCOURT BRACE JOVANOVICH, INC.
NEW YORK

Printed in the United States of America

D E F G H I J K

Library of Congress Cataloging in Publication Data

Cohen, Daniel.
    ESP: the search beyond the senses.

    Bibliography: p.
    SUMMARY: A history of psychic phenomena and
research including many case studies.
    1. Extrasensory perception—Juvenile literature.
[1. Parapsychology.   2. Psychical research.
3. Extrasensory perception]   I. Title.
[DNLM: 1. Parapsychology.   BF1321 C678e 1973]
BF1321.C63   133.8   73-5238
ISBN 0-15-226250-4

To Wolfa

Contents

ESP

What Is ESP?

If you had been thinking about a friend and then you suddenly and unexpectedly got a telephone call from him, you might be tempted to say, "Why, it must be ESP."

If you had a hunch or feeling that something unusual was about to happen and then the thing really did happen, you might think that was ESP, too.

If you had a dream about events that were occurring far away and then later you discovered that the events had taken place just as you had dreamed, that, too, you might attribute to ESP.

ESP or extrasensory perception is no single or simple faculty like hearing or sight; it seems to be a great many things. Please notice I said *seems.* One cannot write about ESP honestly without doing a lot of qualifying. Even those who have committed years of their lives to studying the subject admit that there is a great deal that remains unknown. In describing ESP they constantly use words like "elusive," "a quicksilver ability," and even "frustrating."

The very existence of anything that might be called ESP is highly controversial. Most of those who have conducted extensive ESP experiments are convinced that the existence of extrasensory abilities has been scientifically established, though they might disagree as to the nature of ESP. On the other hand, the vast majority of scientists are not at all convinced, and a sizable percentage, perhaps a majority, seriously doubt if any such thing as ESP is even possible.

In 1955 a survey was conducted among young psychologists, a group that was thought to be exceptionally open-minded about ESP. Only 4 percent thought that ESP was an established fact, while a slightly higher percentage, about 7 percent, believed it to be an impossibility. A whopping 32 percent thought ESP was only a remote possibility. The remainder was divided more or less evenly between thinking that ESP was a likely possibility and having no particular opinion on the subject. A survey of physicists or biologists would probably reveal an even more negative attitude toward ESP.

The scientific community is not just being pigheaded about ESP; their doubts about its existence are perfectly reasonable. We shall examine these doubts in later chapters, but for now let us assume that something called extrasensory perception exists. What do the words mean?

The term extrasensory perception was first popularized by Dr. Joseph Banks Rhine, formerly of Duke

University, one of the most notable of the scientists who have studied the subject. Dr. Rhine, in his book *Extrasensory Perception,* first tentatively defined ESP as "perception without the function of the recognized senses"—that is, somehow being aware of something without touching, hearing, seeing, smelling, or tasting it.

Many have thought of ESP as some sort of mysterious "sixth sense," a form of perception as yet unrecognized by science. But Rhine himself has arrived at a different view. He now defines ESP as "perception in a mode that is just *not* sensory." This second definition raises a major problem, for if ESP is not sensory, what is it? No one is able to give a clear answer to that question.

We will go into the rather sticky problem of whether ESP is a sixth sense or not a sense at all in a later chapter. Right now just keep in mind that even those who study ESP have never really agreed upon a definition for the subject they are studying. Some don't even like the phrase "extrasensory perception" at all. They speak of psychic or psi phenomena. Psychic means beyond the known physical processes. People who study ESP are called parapsychologists (those who study things beyond psychology) and psychical researchers. The best way to find out what ESP is is to look at some of the examples collected by those who have studied the subject.

In *Extrasensory Perception,* Dr. Rhine relates this experience of a family that he knows well: "One day the father was driving home by automobile along a

New Jersey highway. Suddenly, with no warning, he felt a crushing pain, so severe he thought he would die, shoot through his chest. He somehow managed to stop the car. After a short while he recovered. There seemed nothing the matter with him, then he drove home. While telling his wife about this strange experience the like of which he had never had before (nor, for that matter, during the many years that have passed since), and discussing the need for a medical examination, the telephone rang. It was a message stating that his son in Colorado had been killed in a head-on collision of the car which he had been driving. The time of his son's death coincided closely with that of his own violent chest pain. The son was crushed against the wheel."

This experience might be classed as telepathy—the perception of the mental processes or, as in this case, the feeling of another person.

A somewhat different type of ESP seems to be in operation in a case that appeared in the nineteenth century in the Journal of the Society for Psychical Research. The case was outlined in a letter written in 1889 by Sir John Drummond Hay, the British Minister to Morocco.

"In the year 1879 my son Robert Drummond Hay resided at Mogodor with his family, where he was at that time Consul. It was in the month of February. I had lately received good accounts of my son and his family; I was also in perfect health. About 1 A.M. (I forget the exact day in February), whilst sleeping soundly [at Tangier about three hundred miles from

Mogodor] I was woke by hearing distinctly the voice of my daughter-in-law who was with her husband at Mogodor, saying in a clear, but distressed tone of voice, 'Oh I wish papa' only knew that Robert is ill.' There was a night lamp in the room. I sat up and listened, looking around the room, but there was no one except my wife, sleeping quietly in bed. I listened for some seconds, expecting to hear footsteps outside, but complete stillness prevailed, so I lay down again, thanking God that the voice,which woke me was an hallucination. I had hardly closed my eyes when I heard the same voice and words, upon which I woke Lady Drummond Hay and told her what had occurred, and got up and went into my study, adjoining the bedroom, and noted it in my diary. [The diary was later destroyed; that is why Sir Drummond'Hay could not set the exact date.] Next morning I related what had happened to my daughter, saying that, though I did not believe in dreams, I felt anxious for tidings from Mogodor."

Sir Drummond Hay's letter goes on to explain how a few days later he received a letter telling him that his son was seriously ill with typhoid,fever and that his daughter-in-law was deeply worried. Sir Drummond Hay then wrote his daughter-in-law about his dream.

"She replied, the following post, that in her distress at seeing her husband so dangerously ill, and from being alone in a distant land, she had made use of the precise words which had startled me from sleep, and had repeated them. As it may be of interest for you to receive a corroboration of what I had related from the persons I have mentioned, who happen to be with me at this date, they also sign to affirm the accuracy of all I have related."

This experience might be classed as telepathy—Sir Drummond Hay had somehow been in contact with the mind of his daughter-in-law three hundred miles away. Most researchers, however, would look upon this incident as one of clairvoyance, the experience of seeing or otherwise perceiving a distant event or object.

Still a third type of ESP may be in operation in this very dramatic case that was also printed in the official publication of the British Society for Psychical Research:

"Being at length tired, I sat down to rest upon a rock at the edge of the water. My attention was quite taken up with the extreme beauty of the scene before me. There was not a sound of movement except the soft ripple of water on the sand at my feet. Presently I felt a cold chill creep through me, and a curious stiffness of my limbs, as if I could not move though wishing to do so. I felt frightened, yet chained to the spot, and as if impelled to stare at the water straight in front of me. Gradually a black cloud seemed to rise, and in the midst of it I saw a tall man, in a suit of tweed, jump into the water and sink.

"In a moment the darkness was gone, and I again became sensible of the heat and sunshine, but I was awed and felt eerie—it was about four o'clock or so— I cannot remember either the exact time or date. On my sister's arrival I told her of the occurrence; she was surprised, but inclined to laugh at it. When I got home I told my brother; he treated the subject much in the same manner. However, about a week afterwards a Mr. Espie, a bank clerk (unknown to me), committed suicide by drowning in the very spot. He left a letter for his wife, indicating that he had for some time contemplated his death. My sister's memory of the event is the only evidence I can give. I did not see the account of the inquest at the time, and did not mention my strange experience to anyone saving my sister and brother."

It is possible that the writer somehow was in telepathic contact with Mr. Espie before he committed suicide, and the vision he saw was drawn from the doomed clerk's mind. But most people would say that the writer had a premonition, that he foresaw an event that was to take place in the future. In the language of parapsychology, it was a case of precognition.

Telepathy, clairvoyance, and precognition are the three main divisions of ESP, though, as you can see from these cases, the divisions are by no means well defined. It is possible that all of these experiences resulted from different facets of a single unknown ability. There is, however, still more to ESP. If a mind possesses the power to influence another mind over a vast distance, or even through time itself, isn't it possible that this unknown power can also influence physical objects?

Here is a case recorded in 1922 by the early twentieth-century French astronomer Camille Flammarion, who had an abiding interest in psychical research and wrote extensively on the subject.

"One night the bell—the cord of which went from

the alcove where my parents slept, to the nurse's room on the first floor—began to ring loudly.

"In all haste my sister, whose room was next to that of the nurse, went to look for the latter, and both went down to learn if Mother were ill, and why the bell had rung.

"At that very moment they heard the bell ring again. My father sprang from his bed. The bell cord and clapper were still in motion.

"There were thus four witnesses fully awake, and nothing could set the bell in motion save someone in the alcove. Before going back to bed, my father looked at the clock; it was half past two. The night following the next he got a letter from Paris telling him of the death of a relative. It had happened [the bell ringing] at the very night and the very hour his relative had died."

This, say the parapsychologists, might be a case of psychokinesis (often abbreviated as P.K.), or mind over matter.

All of the cases related so far have had something to do with death or serious illness. Not all of the study of ESP is concerned with death, but, as we shall see, parapsychologists are greatly concerned with what happens to a person at the moment of death, and after death. In fact, one of the most controversial, yet compelling, aspects of psychical research is communicating with or seeing the dead.

Psychical researchers have in their files thousands of accounts of what we might call "ghost stories," that is, accounts of people who believe that they had seen or in one manner or another had been in contact with the dead. Here is a fairly typical case collected by pioneer psychical researchers Edmund Gurney and Frederic Myers and published in 1886 in *Phantasms of the Living:*

September 15th, 1886

Dear Sir,—The facts are simply these. I was sleeping in a hotel in Maderia in January 1885. It was a bright moonlight night. The windows were open and the blinds up. I felt someone was in my room. On opening my eyes, I saw a young fellow about 25, dressed in flannels, standing at the side of my bed and pointing with the first finger of his right hand to the place I was lying. I lay for some seconds to convince myself of someone being really there. I sat up and looked at him. I saw his features so plainly that I recognized them in a photograph which was shown to me some days after. I asked him what he wanted; he did not speak, but his eyes and hand seemed to tell me I was in his place. As he did not answer, I struck out at him with my fist and I sat up, but did not reach him, and as I was going to spring out of bed he slowly vanished through the door which was shut, keeping his eyes upon me all the time . . .

John E. Husbands

Gurney and Myers also received letters from a Miss Falkner, who was a resident at the hotel where the incident occurred.

October 8th, 1886

Dear Sir,—The figure that Mr. Husbands saw while in Maderia was that of a young fellow who died unexpectedly months previously, in the room which Mr. Husbands was occupying. Curiously enough, Mr. H. had never heard of him or his death. He told me the story in the morning after he had seen the figure, and I recognized the young fellow from the description. It impressed me very much, but I did not mention it to him or anyone. I loitered about until I heard Mr. Husbands tell the same tale to my brother; we left Mr. H. and said simultaneously "He has seen Mr. D."

No more was said on the subject for days; then I abruptly showed the photograph.

Mr. Husbands said at once, "That is the young fellow who appeared to me the other night, but he was dressed differently"—describing a dress he often wore —"cricket suit (or tennis) fastened at the neck with sailor knot." I must say that Mr. Husbands is a most practical man, and the very last one would expect a spirit to visit.

K. Falkner

October 20th, 1886

Dear Sir,—I enclose a photograph and an extract from my sister-in-law's letter which I received this morning, as it will verify my statement. Mr. Husbands saw the figure either on the 3rd or 4th of February 1885.

The people who had occupied the rooms had never told us if they had seen anything, so we may conclude they had not.

K. Falkner

Closely related to the study of psychokinesis, and possibly to contact with the dead, is the problem of poltergeists, another subject that has fascinated psychical researchers for over a century. The word poltergeist comes from a German expression meaning noisy or boisterous ghost. When a house is suddenly afflicted by strange and inexplicable sounds and small objects seem to be moved about by no known force, this is said to be evidence of the activities of a poltergeist.

A typical poltergeist case took place at Seaford, Long Island, in 1958. The police as well as psychical researchers investigated this case. Here, from the police record, are some of the incidents that were supposed to have taken place:

"At about 1015 hours [10:15 A.M.] the whole family was in the dining room of the house. Noises were heard to come from different rooms and on checking it was found that a holy water bottle on the dresser in the master bedroom had opened and spilled, a new bottle of toilet water on the dresser in the master bedroom had fallen, lost its screw cap and also a rubber stopper, and the contents were spilled. At the same time, a bottle of shampoo and a bottle of Kaopectate in the bathroom had lost the caps and fallen over spilling their contents. The starch in the kitchen was also opened and spilled again and a can of paint thinner in the cellar had opened, fallen and was spilling on the floor."

Neither police nor parapsychologists were ever able to come to any final conclusions about the Seaford poltergeist, though the case was investigated closely.

Another aspect of the study of ESP that seems to involve some as yet unknown connection between mind and matter is psychometry or object reading. In psychometry the subject, usually a person who is known to possess "psychic" powers, will take an object and by handling it be able to determine something about the person who owned the object or who had last handled it.

Dr. Eugene Osty, an early twentieth-century psychical researcher, investigated a French psychometrist called Mme Morel in the early 1920s. As a test Mme Morel was given a book of Esperanto (a proposed international language) and asked to say something about the person to whom it belonged.

Raynor Johnson in his book *Psychical Research* gives us Mme Morel's description of a young man, with peculiar eyes: "Then one day, one morning, he departs with others . . . a long march . . . he then goes in a train. I see him a little later with others in a kind of hole . . . I hear much noise . . . I see fury in his brain; he goes up. . . . What a noise I hear! He feels a blow and falls . . . gets up . . . receives another blow, and falls afresh with others on a road." The psychometrist then went on to describe the death and burial of the young man who had owned the book.

Mr. Johnson also gives us a comment on the psychometrist's account by M. Emile Boriac, who had supplied the book to Dr. Osty:

"The little manual of Esperanto that I gave you was taken from the civilian clothing left at my house by the son of one of my friends. The young man was after-wards a second-lieutenant in the 27th Regiment, killed or missing on December 12th in a trench attack at the Bois-Brule.

"G.M. was aged twenty-five or twenty-six, tall, slight, face rather long, and his eyelids had a slight fold, like the Chinese. . . . As far as is known, he was wounded leading the attack, but continued at the head of his men, then fell at the edge of the German trench which is still in the hands of the enemy."

The lieutenant's body had not been recovered and presumably had been buried by the Germans. M. Boriac commented, "The vision is therefore correct, with some particulars that cannot be ascertained."

In the study of ESP, any phenomenon that hints there are forces or powers outside of the recognized forces of the material world is of interest to the parapsychologists and psychical researchers. They have investigated the apparently extrasensory abilities of some animals and have studied cases of persons who have claimed to be able to "see" with their fingertips. People who say that they can heal or diagnose diseases by psychic power or see "auras" surrounding others have also fallen into the province of ESP investigators. Although some of the work of parapsychologists seems to have little if anything to do with perception, extra-sensory or not, they are not merely trying to find out if man has some yet unrecognized "sixth sense." Their aim is far more ambitious; they are probing the very basic scientific assumptions about how the universe operates.

The examples that have been cited and thousands upon thousands of others that have been collected by psychical researchers throughout the world are known as "spontaneous cases." They are fascinating, weird, and apparently inexplicable by any normal means. Perhaps they are highly significant, but as most psychical researchers will readily admit, spontaneous cases, no matter how strange they seem, will not prove the existence of ESP, at least as far as the bulk of the scientific community is concerned. Such incidents are too loose; there are too many chances for fraud, error, or coincidence. one incident - Relate to paper on GIR

Perhaps the person who said he had a premonition of a man jumping into the water was simply making up an agreeably exotic story. The British civil servant who thought he heard his distant daughter-in-law's voice telling of his son's illness may have been confused about the dates or unconsciously embellished the story after he found out that his son was ill. The man who had severe chest pains at about the same time his son was killed in an accident may have been involved in an unusual coincidence. People make up stories and make mistakes, and odd coincidences do occur. The possibilities of fraud, error, and coincidence must be screened out as much as possible for any event to be labeled as definitely extrasensory. This has been one of the great tasks of parapsychology.

In order to understand the modern study of ESP

and the reason some people are utterly convinced that it exists while others are equally sure it is impossible, we must know how the subject of parapsychology or psychical research developed.

2

Prophets and Visionaries

For centuries no one ever had to prove the existence of ESP simply because very few people ever doubted that such abilities existed. Every society had its prophets. There were always those who seemed to know what others were thinking or what was happening in distant places. One did not even need a special ability to have what we call a "psychic experience"; anyone could have a prophetic dream or see a ghost.

Up until two or three centuries ago, the things that we now call *extra*sensory perception would not have been regarded as extrasensory or extra anything. They were considered a perfectly normal, if not common, part of life. In primitive tribes, for example, the witch doctor or shaman would go into a trance (a sleeplike state), utter prophecies, deliver warnings from the spirits of ancestors, pick out individuals who were guilty of crimes, and perform other acts that would today be classed as psychic.

Many ancient peoples stood in awe of dreams, which were believed to reveal the future or the will of the gods more clearly than anything else. Those who believed in the power of dreams were not just primitive tribesmen either. At least one Egyptian pharaoh attributed his success to instructions he had received from a god during a dream.

The Hebrews detested astrology and the myriad forms of fortune telling that were popular with the Babylonians and other pagans. But they did believe that God revealed his plans in dreams and by prophets. In a famous Old Testament story, King Saul, who had displeased God, was no longer given a guide to the future: "And when Saul inquired of the Lord the Lord answered him not, neither by dreams . . . nor prophets."

The Hebrews, in fact, were considered particularly acute interpreters of dreams. When Pharaoh had a dream that none of his regular wizards or soothsayers could interpret, he called for the Hebrew prisoner Joseph, who revealed that the dream was a warning that Egypt would experience seven good years followed by seven years of famine.

The Roman-Jewish historian Josephus, who lived in the first century of the Christian era, expressed what must have been a common view about the nature of dreams. He believed that during sleep the soul was able to leave the body and travel to distant places through time and even converse with God. Dreams, he thought, were memories of these nightly voyages and should be regarded with utmost seriousness. He wrote: "Let me produce the state of sleep as most evident demonstration of the truth of what I say, wherein souls, when the body does not distract them, have the sweetest rest depending on themselves and conversing with God, by their alliance with him; they then go everywhere, and foretell many futurities before-hand."

The Greeks relied heavily on inspired oracles such as the oracle at Delphi. At this ancient shrine a priestess called the pythoness sat atop a high three-legged stool, went into a trance, and issued prophecies, usually garbled and incomprehensible bits of verse, in response to questions put to her by pilgrims at the shrine. The pythoness's utterances were then "interpreted" by a select group of priests who attended the Delphi temple. Though the prophecies, even after being interpreted by the priests, were generally too vague to be much of a guide for the future, the oracle at Delphi remained for many centuries a place of pilgrimage not only for Greeks, but also for peoples of the entire Mediterranean world. No important undertaking was begun in Greece without some consultation of the oracle at Delphi or of some other prophetic shrine. Whether the kings and generals of the ancient world believed implicitly in the oracles is doubtful. The oracles generally told the powerful what they wanted to hear anyway. The common people, however, certainly believed that the gods revealed the future through oracles. Soldiers might refuse to fight if they had not heard a favorable prediction from the oracle.

In Rome the most famous of the inspired prophets were the sibyls. They were believed to have been an ancient group of prophetesses whose predictions for the future of Rome had been collected in a series of books that were consulted by a special body of priests at times of great national emergency. The sibyls were so highly respected that a variety of later prophetic writings were passed off as "sibylline prophecies" and continued to influence the thoughts and actions of men for centuries.

While the sibyls were without a doubt pagan prophetesses, many Christians also believed in their powers. In the second century after the birth of Christ, a Christian writer, perhaps the celebrated Justin Martyr, expressed his belief in the essential accuracy of sibylline prophecy and tried to excuse the failure of some of the prophecies. He wrote a description of how the sibyl worked, which attributes to her many features that we will see again and again in "sensitives" and "mediums" of later eras.

"Unlike the poets who, after their poems are penned, have power to correct and polish, especially in the way of increasing the accuracy of their verse, she [the sibyl] was filled indeed with prophecy at the time of the inspiration, but as soon as the inspiration ceased, there ceased also the remembrance of all she had said. And this indeed was the cause why some, only, and not all, the meters of the verses of the Sibyl were preserved. . . . And besides all else which they told us as they had heard it from their fathers, they said also that they who took down her prophecies, being illiterate persons, often went quite astray from the accuracy of the meters; and this, they said, was the cause of having want of meter in some of the verses, the prophetess having no remembrance of what she had said, after the possession and inspiration ceased, and the reporters, having, through their lack of education, failed to record the meters with accuracy."

Of this ancient account psychical researcher Dr. Walter Franklin Prince comments, "We recognize the state of trance, amnesia of what is said in trance, the claim to predict which in some cases is made impressive by subsequent events, and the urge with a few mediums to present in literary form . . ."

There may seem to be a world of difference between "inspired" prophets like the sibyls and those who believe that they can tell the future by astrology, card reading, and the like. Actually the difference is not as great as it appears. Astrologers and card readers were commonly believed to possess a faculty that we would today call extrasensory. Given the proper training and information, anyone should be able to work out a horoscope, but good astrologers are supposed to be able to see things in the horoscope chart that others cannot.

An art like crystal gazing has been regarded as almost purely "psychic." The crystal itself has no special power; it is merely a means by which the sensitive is able to focus his or her attention and thus get a clearer psychic impression. A person lacking the psychic gift might gaze into the crystal endlessly without seeing a thing. Traditionally, such psychic gifts were thought to be hereditary. The seventh son of a seventh son was credited with the ability to see the future in the crystal ball. Seven was considered a magic number, and in ancient times prophecy and magic were almost inseparable.

Prophecy or precognition is only one form, admittedly a spectacular and popular one, of extrasensory perception that was recorded in past ages. Almost as widespread was the ability to have visions. To the modern parapsychologist, vision is a decidedly unsatisfactory term, for it may mean seeing the future or seeing distant events, but it also may mean seeing other things that most people are unable to see, such as spirits, angels, devils, or fairies. A person possessed of visionary powers, according to popular lore, might do any or all of these things.

Saintly men and women often saw visions of angels who inspired them and even more often of devils who tormented them. People believed that these spiritual creatures populated an invisible world that surrounded their own. From the life of St. Anthony written about the year A.D. 360, we learn that the saint saw devils in many guises. Often they came as black men or giants. But they also appeared to him as "a beast like to man having legs and feet like those of an ass" and as leopards, bears, horses, wolves, and scorpions. "The lion was roaring, wishing to attack, the bull seeming to toss with its horns, the serpent writhing." The shapes of the dove and the lamb—holy symbols—were forbidden. Devils frequently changed shape, "taking the forms of women, wild beasts, creeping things, gigantic bodies, and troops of soldiers . . . at another time they assumed the appearance of monks and feigned the speech of holy men." The most feared shape assumed by the demons was that of an angel. This was the dreaded "midday devil" mentioned in the Psalms. The frequency with which demons were supposed to appear as angels caused St. Mary a great deal of anxiety at the Annunciation.

Some holy men saw demons everywhere. According to St. Macarius of Alexandria, devils were "as numerous as bees," while the Blessed Reichhelm of Schongan, who lived at the end of the thirteenth century, compared their numbers to drops of rain or the specks of dust one can see in a sunbeam. He was unusually exact for a visionary, for he computed that there were exactly 1,754,064,176 demons in the world.

It wasn't only medieval Catholic saints who saw demons either. Martin Luther reputedly became so irritated by a persistent devil that he threw his inkpot at the fiend.

Angels were less commonly seen or heard, and because of the frequency with which devils were supposed to appear as angels, an angelic vision could be dangerous. The most celebrated example of the dangers of such visions were the voices and visions that guided Joan of Arc to her victories over the English in the fifteenth century.

After Joan was betrayed and brought to trial by the church, she was questioned closely about her visions. At her trial, in response to a question of whether she saw St. Michael and the angels corporeally, Joan replied, "I see them with my own corporeal eyes, as well as I see you. And when they leave I weep, and I wish they would take me with them." Her accusers claimed that these saints and angels were really devils.

The story of the Maid of Orleans is so dramatic that it has inspired thousands of books. But psychical researchers have also taken a great interest in this case, for they regard the career of Joan of Arc as one of the best attested historical examples of some sort of psychic ability in action.

Psychical researcher Walter Franklin Prince writes: "Putting aside all that is doubtful, there remains a series of astounding facts, part of which are vindicated by irrefutable documents and by competent and responsible witnesses, and a part of which today rest solely on the word of one who as fully deserves her canonization as a saint as anyone who ever walked the earth. If she was a hysteric, it is a pity that the formula by which such hysteria may be induced could not be learned by others, so that they too could become superwomen. If she was insane, it was an insanity which gave her ability, without instruction, to wage war so as to amaze trained leaders, to tutor princes and dominate military councils, to be a match for the combined learning and skill of a throng of ecclesiastical lawyers for several terrible weeks. If she was a fanatic, it was a fanaticism which is the glory of France and has filled the world with memorials in her honor."

Joan was, as everyone knows, burned at the stake for what she did. Her accusers did not say that her voices and visions were imaginary. The real dispute was over whether these voices were divine or diabolical in origin. In the indictment against her, Joan was "denounced and declared sorceress, witch, diviner, pseudo-prophetess, invoker of evil spirits, conjurer, superstitious, implicated in and given to the arts of magic, doubting the Catholic faith, schismatic . . ."

The spiritual beings that appeared to the eyes of visionaries were not only called devils and angels. In parts of Europe these spirits were often called by the names of fairies, elves, pixies, or any of a huge variety of local variations. Though the idea of "fairy tales" is something of a joke today, for hundreds of years people believed very sincerely in the existence of "the little people." There was much talk of fairies at the trial of Joan of Arc. There were numerous theories about the origins of fairies; often it was believed that they were a race of spirits and could only be seen by those who possessed "second sight." Here is a fairly typical account that was collected by Walter Yeeling Evans-Wentz during the nineteenth century from a Mrs. Catherine Jones, an elderly Welsh woman, who had the reputation of being a seeress.

"I was coming home at about half-past ten at night from Cemas, on the path to Simdda Wen, where I was in service, when there appeared just before me a very pretty young lady of ordinary size. [These "little people" according to many legends, were really quite large.] I had no fear, and when I came up to her put out my hand to touch her, but my hand and arm went right through her form. I could not understand this, and so tried to touch her repeatedly with the same result; there was no solid substance in the body, yet it remained beside me, and was as beautiful a young lady as I ever saw. When I reached the door of the house where I was to stop, she was still with me. Then I said 'Good night' to her. No response being made, I asked, 'Why do you not speak?' And at this she disappeared. Nothing happened afterwards, and I always put this beautiful young lady down as one of the *Tylwyth Teg* [a race of spirits in Welsh folklore]."

In addition to prophecy and visions, saints and others occasionally displayed a really spectacular form of psychokinesis—that is, levitation. The early Christians told of how an evil wizard named Simon Magus flew through the air during a dispute with St. Peter, but that the saint cut him down in mid-flight with a well-aimed prayer. This and many other stories of levitation from India, portions of the Orient, and Africa, as well as Europe, are common enough, but we have nothing in the way of reliable records to back them up.

In the case of the seventeenth-century Italian holy man St. Joseph of Copertino, however, there is a large body of testimony that is not so easily ignored. St. Joseph, according to most accounts, was a rather simple-minded monk, who was much addicted to asceticism and extreme mortification of the flesh. His self-inflicted tortures would be considered pathological in our day and were regarded as extreme even in his own time. Joseph's superiors often had to restrain him from whipping himself and from wearing barbed metal next to his skin. He regularly fell into ecstatic raptures where he was entirely senseless, and according to many stories, it was while in such states that St. Joseph not only levitated but actually flew.

One of the saint's more impressive flights was reported to have taken place during the visit of a Spanish nobleman and his wife. The nobleman's wife and her retinue of women expressed the strong wish to see the famous friar. But Joseph was adverse to the idea since he avoided women on all possible occasions. However, his superiors insisted that he visit the women in the church. Joseph said that he would, but did not know if he would be able to speak. So the unwilling friar left his cell and entered the church full of women. The first object Joseph saw was a statue of the Immaculate Conception. Upon seeing this, Joseph uttered a cry, rose into the air, and flew over to the statue. There he remained for some time in a state of speechless adoration. Then he uttered another shriek, flew back to the door, bowed to the Mother of God, kissed the ground, and, with his head inclined and cowl lowered, hastened back to his cell. Behind him he left a group of ladies fainting with amazement over what they had seen.

In addition to his frequent levitations, Joseph was credited with other psychic abilities. When he acted as confessor, he was often said to read the thoughts of those who were confessing to him. Joseph once asked a doctor who was attending him whether he had made his confession. The doctor replied that he had, but Joseph countered, "Go and think a little more." The doctor reflected for a moment but said he could remember nothing. Then Joseph told him to think of what he was doing on a certain day at a certain hour. This jogged the doctor's memory, and he quickly confessed the forgotten fault.

Claims for the ability to levitate are not common today, but throughout the late nineteenth and early twentieth centuries, leading spirit mediums regularly performed what they called levitations during their seances.

Today people who regularly see ghosts are thought of as being either psychic or crazy, but in the past people believed in ghosts so strongly that seeing one was not considered unusual. So powerful was the belief in ghosts, that they actually served a useful social purpose. One seventeenth-century Englishman wrote that ghosts were active "in detecting their murderer, in disposing of their estate, in rebuking injurious executors, in visiting and counselling their wives and children, in forewarning them of such and such courses, with other matters of like sort."

History records numerous examples such as the English account of the ghost of a man named Fletcher, which appeared around 1624 to haunt his wife's lover who had been responsible for his murder. The haunting so terrified the murderer that he confessed to his crime, whereas he would otherwise have gone scot-free.

In 1679 London street salesmen hawked a pamphlet, the title of which speaks for itself: *Strange and Wonderful news from Lincolnshire. Or a Dreadful Account of a Most Inhuman and Bloody Murther, committed upon the Body of one Mr. Carter by the Contrivance of his elder Brother, who had hired three more villains to commit the Horrid Fact, and how it was soon after found out by the Appearance of a Most Dreadful and Terrible Ghost, sent by Almighty Providence for the Discovery.*

By the latter half of the eighteenth century, educated people had begun to express nagging doubts about all accounts of supernatural activities. Still an unusually well-authenticated case would excite considerable interest even among rationalist intellectuals. Such a case, or series of cases, was attached to the life of the Swedish scientist and religious mystic Emanuel Swedenborg.

Swedenborg, who was an extremely respected and respectable individual, claimed that he could go into trances and visit the spirit world. As a result of the revelations he received from the spirits, he wrote a series of weighty and dull volumes of theology. But what attracted most attention was the various feats of extrasensory perception attributed to the Swedish seer.

His most famous accomplishment (and still one of the most interesting examples of alleged clairvoyance in all history) was Swedenborg's observation of the progress of a fire that was taking place well over two hundred miles away. In September of 1759 Swedenborg was staying with a party of about fifteen people at the town of Göteborg. Here is an excerpt from the most complete description of the incident:

"At about six o'clock, Swedenborg went out, and returned to the company quite pale and alarmed. He said that a dangerous fire had just broken out in Stockholm at Sodermalm [about two hundred and forty miles northeast of Göteborg] and that it was spreading very fast. He was restless, and he went out often. He said that the house of one of his friends, whom he named, was already in ashes, and that his own was in danger. At eight o'clock, he had been out again, he joyfully exclaimed, 'Thank God! the fire is extinguished, the third door from my house!' The news occasioned great commotion throughout the city, but particularly amongst the company in which he was. It was announced to the governor the same evening. On Sunday morning Swedenborg was summoned to the governor, who questioned him concerning the disaster."

It was not until two days after the events described by Swedenborg that the people of Göteborg actually received information by messenger that a fire had broken out in Stockholm, just exactly as Swedenborg had reported.

These incidents are a mere sampling, chosen almost at random from the huge catalog of strange and possibly psychic or extrasensory experiences that have been recorded throughout history. People might disagree as to whether this or that event had indeed taken place as described, or whether it had been embellished along the way to make a more interesting story. They certainly disagreed as to the cause of any particular phenomena. St. Joan and her supporters asserted that her voices and visions were divinely inspired, whereas her opponents denounced them as the devil's handiwork. Some of her opponents doubtless either did not believe in her visions at all or didn't much care about them. They merely used the charge of diabolical inspiration in order to get a dangerous opponent burned. But to the common people and probably to the majority of nobles and clergy as well, the visions and voices were real, and the problem of whether they were divine or diabolical was a real and important one.

This confusion between divine and diabolical was even more sharply drawn in the case of Magdalena de la Cruz. Magdalena was an early sixteenth-century abbess at Cordova in Spain. Like St. Joseph of Copertino, she was reported to fall into raptures during which she floated above the ground. In addition, she showed evidence of being clairvoyant and telepathic.

In 1534 the saintly abbess fell sick, and it seemed as if she was going to die. She confessed that since the age of five she had been under the control of demons, and it was the demons who had helped her to perform the miracles that had been observed as occurring during her raptures. Those who heard Magdalena were horrified, and perhaps if she had died at that time, the world would never have known of her confession. But she recovered, and her confession was investigated in some detail. The investigators finally concluded that she was indeed in the possession of a demon, and she was then moved to another convent where she was placed under strict discipline. She died in 1560.

So long as people accepted the possibility of such things as prophetic dreams, second sight, and levitation, there seemed little reason for investigating any particular claim too closely. The existence of such phenomena seemed to be attested to by such an overpowering quantity of evidence gathered from all times and all places that doubt was well nigh impossible. Yet, even in the seventeenth century a small trickle of doubt concerning these apparently miraculous events began to appear. By the eighteenth century the trickle had grown to a torrent, at least among the educated.

The reason for the growing skepticism about extrasensory phenomena was the increasing respectability of science and the scientific method. Such things as levitation simply did not fit into the scheme of the world as it was being revealed by science. In addition, the scientific method would not be satisfied by an appeal to tradition. Just because everybody had believed in a particular thing for thousands of years did not necessarily mean that the thing was true. After all, for thousands of years people had attested to the existence of such creatures as the unicorn and the griffin, and yet these creatures did not exist.

Stronger evidence than mere tradition had to be marshaled in order to support the existence of these strange occurrences, and upon closer investigation the evidence often turned out to be disconcertingly thin. There was, of course, no way of checking out the accuracy of accounts that were centuries old. But even accounts of recent psychic events proved to be not so well documented as the scientifically minded would have liked.

Take, for example, the story of Emanuel Swedenborg's clairvoyant description of the fire in Stockholm. This story was repeated all over Europe and finally came to the attention of the German philosopher Immanuel Kant. Kant was intrigued. In 1767, some eight years after Swedenborg's reputed demonstration of clairvoyance, Kant asked a friend of his named Green who was traveling to Sweden "to make particular inquiries respecting the miraculous gift which Swedenborg possesses." Green interviewed a number of people and repeated their stories to Kant, who wrote up the most complete existing report of the incident. Unfortunately, most of those whom Green interviewed seem to have heard of the event at second or third hand. The only eyewitness to the incident whom Green is known to have interviewed was Swedenborg himself. As a result, Kant remained doubtful about Swedenborg's abilities.

So it was that by the beginning of the nineteenth century, all of those phenomena that we now call extrasensory were not only doubted, but were denounced as relics of a superstitious and credulous age. At first, the questions had been raised only by a relative handful of intellectuals. But as time wore on, more and more people began to question the ancient beliefs. The result was a genuine crisis of faith. If one did not believe that such things as prophecy, clairvoyance, and communication with the dead existed, indeed could exist at all, it was a short stop to doubting the existence of man's immortal soul and of God Himself. It was out of this painful crisis of faith that psychical research was born.

3

The Beginnings of Psychical Research

Frederic Myers, a pioneer of psychical research, once remarked that the most important question one could ask was, "Is the universe friendly?" Most of those who helped to start the organized investigation of psychical subjects during the last quarter of the nineteenth century were troubled by just such a question, and this was the sort of uncertainty that lay behind the foundations of modern psychical research.

For some centuries scientists seemed to have been suggesting that the universe was neither friendly nor unfriendly to mankind, just supremely and horribly indifferent. Astronomers had demoted the earth from the center of the universe to a minor planet circling a very ordinary star. Physicists and chemists had begun to reveal a universe that operated not by the will of a divine being, but by mathematically precise and coldly impersonal laws. Geologists had cast serious doubts on some of the stories in the Bible, particularly the story of the universal flood. In 1851, the British essayist John Ruskin wrote in a letter to a friend: "If only those geologists would let me alone, I could do very well, but those dreadful hammers. I hear the clink of them at the end of every cadence of the Bible verses."

During the 1850s the science of physiology began to demonstrate that mental changes were accompanied by changes in the brain. These discoveries made it possible to suggest that such spiritual qualities as intellect and will might really be the result of the physical qualities of brain tissue.

Most of these discoveries created only minor, though irritating, ripples in the great and placid pool of religious certainty that marked early Victorian England. During the first half of the nineteenth century it was still possible to believe that science and religion were allies and that ultimately science would prove a more effective way of revealing the workings and the will of an all knowing and benevolent God. True, the religion of nineteenth century England in no way resembled the passionate Christianity of earlier centuries, but it was certainly possible for man to believe that the universe was not only friendly but also progressive.

Then came the year 1859 and the publication of Charles Darwin's *On the Origin of Species*. This book was shocking enough. The shock was compounded in 1871 when Darwin followed with an even more disturbing work, *The Descent of Man*. The accumulated effect of Darwin's two books and those of his followers was shattering to the religious tranquillity of the edu-

cated Christian of Victorian England and to his coun-
terpart in the United States.

In *On the Origin of Species,* Darwin seemed to be
directly attacking the account of creation as set down
in the Bible. According to Darwin, creatures evolved
by an almost accidental process called "natural selec-
tion." There was no mention of "God's plan"; in fact,
God was left out entirely.

And there was more. In *The Descent of Man* Darwin
attacked the whole idea that man had a moral sense
derived directly from God. Morality, he contended,
could differ greatly under different conditions: "If, for
instance, to take an extreme case, men were reared
under precisely the same conditions as hive bees, there
can hardly be a doubt that our unmarried females
would, like the worker bees, think it a sacred duty to
kill their brothers, and mothers would strive to kill
their fertile daughters, and no one would think of inter-
fering."

Educated Englishmen of Queen Victoria's time re-
acted to this cold and impersonal universe that was
presented to them more in anguish than in anger. As
much as they didn't like what the Darwinians and
others were saying, they found it impossible to dismiss
the dreadful ideas out of hand, for Darwin had amassed
a great body of evidence to support his argument. The
educated English Christian was committed to the
scientific method. Science and technology had brought
unheard-of prosperity to the Western world, and particularly to England. Science had freed men's minds
from many of the ancient fears and medieval super-

stitions that had so long afflicted them. No reasonable mid-nineteenth-century Englishman could reject the enormous power of science, but now it seemed that science had gone too far and was about to overthrow traditional religion and morality and leave man entirely adrift. "It is said that in the tropical forests one can almost hear the vegetation growing," wrote one distressed Englishman in 1877. "One may almost say that with us one can hear the faith decaying."

Could the apparent breach between science on the one hand and traditional religion and morality on the other somehow be healed? One development seemed to offer some hope that a friendlier and more personal universe might yet be discovered if only science would trouble to examine it. The development was the movement called modern spiritualism. The basic tenent of spiritualism was that there existed certain individuals called mediums, sensitives, or instruments who could go into trances and, while entranced, get in touch with the spirits of the dead or at least some sort of spirits "in the world beyond." These spirits would then either speak through the medium or perform any number of other strange and wondrous acts by employing their "spirit power." There was nothing really new about spiritualism. The use of entranced mediums to receive messages from some sort of spirit world had been common for thousands of years. Though the practice had fallen into some disrepute in Europe and America, it still went on under a variety of names during the nineteenth century.

The incident that set off the explosion of modern

spiritualism took place in 1848 in the little village of Hydsville, New York, near Rochester. A house inhabited by the Fox family was afflicted by a series of unexplained knockings or rappings. Two young sisters who lived in the house, Kate and Maggie Fox, said that the rappings were caused by the spirit of a peddler who had been murdered and buried in the house. The rappings were supposed to be a sort of code by which this spirit could communicate with the living.

From this rather simple beginning modern spiritualism expanded in the most astonishing way. Very soon dozens and ultimately thousands of individuals throughout the world began professing mediumistic powers.

In a typical nineteenth-century seance (a meeting held for the purpose of invoking the dead), a group of people including a medium would gather in a room. The lights would be turned low or turned out entirely. Then all manner of things might begin to happen. A table might move, a cold wind might blow through the room, and strange sounds might be heard coming, apparently from nowhere. Sometimes a glowing and ghostly form would appear in the darkened room and talk to those present. At other times the medium would go into a trance and deliver messages from the spirit world.

Essentially the quality or type of phenomena produced at spiritualist seances was not very different from what had been reported in thousands upon thousands of accounts of spontaneous experiences. Indeed, most of the seance room phenomena were a good deal less impressive than the best of the spontaneous experience reports. But spiritualism did offer one tremendous advantage to those who wished to find evidence of a nonmaterial world—the phenomena were reasonably regular and open to investigation.

If a person reported seeing an apparition or ghost or having a prophetic dream, one either believed the story or rejected it. There was no way of repeating the experience in front of witnesses or otherwise producing spontaneous phenomena on demand. For this reason the scientifically-minded of the eighteenth and nineteenth centuries rejected such stories entirely (no matter how much they would liked to have believed them). In spiritualism, however, one could attend a seance and observe the phenomena first hand. And that is just exactly what many educated persons of the mid-nineteenth and early twentieth centuries did.

Now it would be quite wrong to give the impression that all scientists went rushing off to seances in the hopes of finding evidence of the spirit world. The majority, then as now, were untroubled by the implications of their findings and regarded activities such as spiritualism as silly and quite beyond the realm of serious interest. They were particularly unimpressed by the trivial nature of most "spiritualistic communications."

When the great biologist Thomas Henry Huxley was asked by the London Dialectical Society to join a committee to investigate spiritualistic phenomena, he penned a caustic reply:

". . . supposing the phenomena to be genuine—they

do not interest me. If anybody would endow me with the faculty of listening to the chatter of old women and curates in the nearest cathedral town, I should decline the privilege, having better things to do.

"And if the folk in the spiritual world do not talk more wisely and sensibly than their friends report them to do, I put them in the same category.

"The only good that I can see in a demonstration of the truth of 'Spiritualism' is to furnish an additional argument against suicide. Better live a crossing-sweeper than die and be made to talk twaddle by a 'medium' hired at a guinea a seance."

Huxley's obstinate refusal even to investigate the claims of spiritualism has often been cited by psychical researchers as a perfect example of scientific pighead-edness. But not all scientists were as scornful as Huxley. The great physicist Michael Faraday investigated the popular spiritualistic phenomena called table turning. In table turning (or tipping) a group of persons sit around a table, lightly touching it with their hands. They then ask questions, and the table is supposed to move, apparently under the influence of the spirits who answer the questions. The practice became so popular in England in the 1850s that it was common for hostesses to issue invitations for "tea and table tipping."

Sometimes the answers the table gave seemed suspiciously influenced by the opinions of the sitters. Milbourne Christopher, a magician, in his book *ESP, Seers & Psychics,* tells us of an incident that took place in the home of Rev. E. Gillson, a strict Protestant minister. The group was conversing with a soul that expected to go to hell. The following questions were asked:

" 'Where are Satan's headquarters? Are they in England?' There was a slight movement.

" 'Are they in France?' A violent movement.

" 'Are they in Spain?' Similar agitation.

" 'Are they at Rome?' The table seemed literally frantic."

Faraday devised a number of ingenious experiments to test the spiritual power that was allegedly moving the table. In the end he concluded that the motive power for the table was not in the spirits but in the people who sat around it. Not that anyone had to deliberately move the table (though that was certainly done on many occasions); in most cases the table was moved because of "mechanical pressure exerted inadvertently by the turner."

A really vexing problem in the investigation of spiritualism was that the field was riddled with frauds, and exposures of these frauds were both numerous and embarrassing. A person might find himself praising the power of a medium on one day, only to discover the next that the very same medium had been detected in some shabby bit of fakery.

In 1878 a group of eminent spiritualists conducted what they believed to be careful investigations of a medium called Williams. They were satisfied that the phenomena produced had been absolutely genuine, and they said so in print. Just a few months later

Williams and his new partner, a man named Rita, were caught red-handed in trickery during a seance in Amsterdam.

Not only were Williams and Rita shown to be fakers, but fakers who were so obvious and crude that it was hard to believe that any halfway intelligent person could have been taken in by them in the first place. During the Amsterdam seance one of the sitters became excited and reached up to grab the spirit form of "Charlie" by the coat collar. Instead he found that he was holding Rita's collar. When the mediums were searched, they were found to be carrying some items for which no innocent explanation was available.

In Rita's pockets were found a false beard and a bottle of phosphorized oil, which looked very much like "Charlie's spirit lamp" that had glowed so mysteriously in the dark. William's extra-large pockets revealed a dirty black beard and several yards of very dirty muslin together with a bottle of phosphorized oil. Taken together, these items could easily have been the makeup for the spirit of a repentant pirate called John King who appeared regularly at the seances of Williams and many other mediums.

True believers in spiritualism refused to be put off even by this exposure. Some suggested that the incriminating evidence had been planted by "evil spirits." Others said that the spirits themselves had brought the muslin and other items in order to save themselves the trouble of actually materializing. One spiritualist announced that before he would believe that Williams was dishonest, he would have to consult "John King" himself. Most spiritualists did not carry their rationalizations quite that far. Rather than deny dishonesty entirely, they claimed that faking on this occasion did not automatically mean that other mediums were fakers, or even that these particular mediums faked their phenomena all of the time. Most commonly in cases like this one, spiritualists asserted that any evidence of fakery was the result of an unusual incident and that on many other occasions the very same medium had displayed phenomena that were "undoubtedly genuine."

After a few experiences like the one with Williams and Rita (and such cases were depressingly common), it is not hard to see how honest and intelligent people were driven away from any contact with spiritualism, no matter how much they may have wished to believe its claims. Only the credulous, those who were willing to excuse anything in order to believe, were left behind to observe the progress of the seances. In fact, there were so many sensational exposures of spiritualism that the subject became something of a joke, and it was potentially dangerous for a person's reputation to become identified with it. So despite the enormous popularity of spiritualism, it made relatively few prominent converts, though many prominent people were privately interested in the subject, and there were surprisingly few sustained attempts to investigate the claims of spiritualists.

A notable and welcome exception to the general

reluctance of responsible people to deal with spiritualism and allied subjects was shown by an informal
grouping of English scholars more or less under the
leadership of Henry Sidgwick, professor of philosophy
at Cambridge. Sidgwick and most of his associates had
come from deeply religious backgrounds but had been
driven to reluctant skepticism by the findings of science. Through the investigation of the "spiritual phenomena," they hoped to be able to find their way back
to some sort of faith, if not to orthodox Christianity,
then at least to a belief in a "friendly universe."

Sidgwick and his wife and some of their friends were
very active in the informal investigation of spiritualism
during the late 1860s and 1870s. They attended a great
number of seances, with most of the leading mediums
in England. In the end they were almost always disappointed by what they found or failed to find. Yet
they continued to hope that their investigations might
ultimately prove fruitful.

In 1882 the Society for Psychical Research (SPR)
was organized, and Henry Sidgwick was elected its
first president. The group contained some very prominent members from nearly every field. There was a
past prime minister of England, W. E. Gladstone.
Gladstone praised psychical research as "the most important work which is being done in the world. By far
the most important." A future prime minister, Arthur
Balfour, was a particular friend of Sidgwick's and an
active supporter of the SPR. There were eight Fellows
of the Royal Society, at that time the most prestigious

scientific society in the world. The essayist John Ruskin and the poet Alfred, Lord Tennyson were members of the SPR, as was Charles Lutwidge Dodgson, better known as Lewis Carroll. Also among the membership, said a historian of psychical research, were "a surprising number of titled persons, some of whom were perhaps more decorative than distinguished."

Most of the work, however, was done by a small group, primarily Sidgwick and his friends.

In addition to the study of the phenomena associated with spiritualism, the SPR also set out to investigate such things as thought reading or telepathy, hypnotism, apparitions, haunted houses, and poltergeists.

The investigation of spirit mediums remained frustrating, and after a while some of the SPR members turned away from it in discouragement and disgust. But some of the other investigations seemed to show great promise. Shortly after the SPR was founded, Sidgwick introduced a report of the Committee on Thought Reading by proclaiming:

"We must drive the objector into the position of being forced either to admit the phenomena as inexplicable, at least by him, or to accuse the investigators either of lying or cheating or of a blindness or forgetfulness incompatable with any intellectual condition except absolutely idiocy.

"I am glad to say that this result, in my opinion, has been satisfactorily attained in the investigation of thought reading. Professor Barrett [William Barrett, professor of physics and chairman of the Committee on

Thought Reading] will now bring before you a report which I hope will be only the first of a long series of similar reports which may have reached the same point of conclusiveness."

Unfortunately, the usually careful Sidgwick had put his foot firmly in his mouth with that statement. The report concerned the apparently telepathic abilities of five young daughters of an English clergyman, the Reverend A. M. Creery. Six years later the Creery sisters and a young servant in the house were caught using a code during a similar investigation of their "telepathic powers." They then admitted to having cheated during the earlier tests as well.

The next important investigations carried out by the Committee on Thought Reading were with George Albert Smith and Douglas Blackburn, two young men who could apparently read each other's thoughts under the most stringent experimental conditions. The blindfolded Smith could receive words, and even complex drawings, apparently by extrasensory means from the mind of Blackburn. One of the most impressive tests was later described by Blackburn in the *Daily News*, published in London, September 1, 1911:

"These were the conditions. Smith sat in a chair at the large table. His eyes were padded with wool, and, I think, a pair of folded kid gloves, and bandaged with a thick dark cloth. His ears were filled with one layer of cotton-wool, then pellets of putty. His entire body and the chair in which he sat were enveloped in two very heavy blankets. I remember, when he emerged triumphant he was wet with perspiration, and the paper on which he had successfully drawn the figure was so moist that it broke during the examination by the delighted observers. Beneath his feet and surrounding his chair were thick, soft rugs, rightly intended to deaden and prevent signals by foot shuffles. Smith being rendered contact proof and perfectly insulated, my part began.

"At the farther side of the room—a very large dining room—Mr. Myers showed me, with every precaution, the drawing that I was to transmit to the brain beneath the blankets. It was a tangle of heavy black lines, interlaced, some curved, some straight, the sort of thing an infant playing with a pencil might produce, and I am certain absolutely indescribable in words, let alone in code. I took it, fixed my gaze on it, pacing the room meanwhile and going through the usual process of impressing the figure upon my retina and brain, but always keeping out of touching distance with Smith. These preliminaries occupied perhaps ten or more minutes, for we made a point of never hurrying. I drew and redrew many times openly in the presence of the observers, in order, as I explained and they allowed, to fix it on my brain."

To the members of the SPR Committee on Thought Reading the Smith-Blackburn tests seemed proof positive of the existence of some form of extrasensory mind-to-mind communication. However, when some scientists from outside of the society observed the tests, they became suspicious. One tried to improve the effectiveness of the blindfold and earplugs. After he had done so, tests showed "not the smallest response on the part of Mr. S to Mr. B's volitional endeavours."

Still the results were accepted as genuine by most of the membership of the SPR, and both Smith and Blackburn joined the organization. Smith actually worked for the group by acting as Edmund Gurney's secretary until Gurney's apparent suicide in 1888. He was also instrumental in bringing a series of supposedly telepathic individuals to the attention of the society.

Then in 1908, in an article that appeared in *John Bull,* Blackburn announced that the whole thing had been a hoax: "I am the sole survivor of that group of experimentalists, and as no harm can be done to anyone, but possible good to the cause of truth, I, with mingled feelings of regret and satisfaction now declare that the whole of these alleged experiments were bogus, and originated in the honest desire of two youths to show how easily men of scientific mind and training could be deceived when seeking for evidence in support of a theory they were wishful to establish."

Blackburn asserted that he had started by attempting to expose the tricks of fraudulent mediums. Then he met Smith, and between them they worked up a thought-reading act. Smith was an accomplished hypnotist and often performed in public. They were soon contacted by two of the leading members of the SPR and "saw in them only a superior type of spiritualistic crank." So they set out to fool the SPR. He said they were able to deceive the investigators with tricks they had worked up in just a few weeks. "What are the chances of succeeding inquirors being more successful against 'sensitives' who have had the advantage of more years' experience than Smith and I had weeks?" Blackburn's first exposé attracted little attention, and he wrote a more complete account for the *Daily News* in 1911.

How had the picture transference with the blankets and blindfold been carried off? According to Blackburn, the method was fairly simple. While pacing about the room, he also secretly copied the drawing on a piece of cigarette paper. This he rolled up and put inside the tube of his mechanical pencil. When this was done, he stumbled on the rug near Smith's chair. That was the signal that all was ready.

From under the blankets Smith shouted, "I have it," meaning he had received the impression of the drawing, and stuck his hand out and fumbled around the table saying, "Where's my pencil?" Blackburn handed him his own pencil, the one with the cigarette paper inside.

Under the blankets Smith took out a concealed luminous slate, pushed the bandage off of one of his eyes, and proceeded to copy the drawing from the cigarette paper. When he was finished, he threw back the blankets and pushed back the eye bandage (so that no one would notice it had been moved already), and presented the copy to the delighted SPR investigators.

Blackburn, who had been out of England for some time, was mistaken in thinking he was the "sole survivor" of the experiment. His partner Smith was very much alive and now denied all of Blackburn's allegations. Blackburn retorted by challenging Smith to prove his telepathic powers again. This Smith declined to do. Today psychical researchers are divided over whether the Smith-Blackburn tests are to be dismissed as a series of hoaxes or not. Professional magicians have performed far more difficult feats, and Smith was at least a semiprofessional performer. It must be admitted that Blackburn and Smith could have cheated, and as long as that is possible, the tests cannot be in any way regarded as conclusive. It has even been hinted that Edmund Gurney, one of the principal investigators and Smith's employer, had discovered evidence of the fraud and was so shocked that it drove him to suicide. No one really knows.

The unsuccessful investigations of the Creery sisters and of Smith and Blackburn are only one side of the picture. Blackburn claimed that it was particularly easy to fool someone who wished to believe in the phenomena. The career of Richard Hodgson proves that such was not always the case. Hodgson was born in Australia in 1855 and studied law there, but he was more attracted to philosophy, so he came to England, where he met Sidgwick and fell under his influence. As a young man Hodgson had been a fervent Methodist, but like so many others, he had reluctantly come to doubt the religious precepts with which he had been raised. Still he admitted that he always possessed a strong desire to believe. That is why, when he was offered full-time employment with the SPR, he accepted, though the pay was far lower than he could have obtained in other fields. Ultimately, he came to America, where he headed the American branch of the SPR until his death in 1905. In the years before his death Hodgson became completely converted to spiritualism after working with the American medium Mrs. Lenora Piper, whom he was convinced was genuine.

If anyone was ready to be fooled, it would appear to have been Richard Hodgson, but quite the reverse was true. Hodgson's first assignment as an SPR investigator was to go to India to check the claims of Madame Helena P. Blavatsky, a Russian adventuress who had started a religion called theosophy. Madame Blavatsky regularly produced a variety of "miracles" for her thousands of devoted followers. After a few months of investigation Hodgson concluded that she was a fraud, though originally he had tended to believe many of her claims. His report for the SPR was so devastating that it virtually destroyed Madame Blavatsky's credibility among scientifically minded psychical investigators. It did not, however, destroy theosophy, which still exists, and modern theosophists are to this day writing angry diatribes denouncing Hodgson.

Hodgson became an expert at conjuring tricks and was the terror of fraudulent mediums. It was largely through his efforts that Eusapia Palladino, the most flamboyant and colorful medium of her day, was first exposed. Hodgson's exposures of fraud were so frequent and ferocious that some of his colleagues charged that he was running the society *against* psychical research, and he was never really popular. But, in truth,

Richard Hodgson ardently wished to see the reality of the psychical phenomena proven, but he wanted it to be proven honestly, and he hated frauds more sincerely and passionately than did the skeptics.

One of Hodgson's more successful efforts was against the practice of slate writing. In the 1880s a number of mediums claimed that during seances they could induce the spirits to write out messages on little blackboards or slates. Sometimes the mediums would hold the slate under the table when the message was written; at times the slate was supposed to be locked up during the seance, and the message was seen only after the slate was unlocked. There were a variety of slate writing techniques, but the whole practice smelled strongly of sleight of hand as Hodgson pointed out in an article. Still many people were impressed, and slate writing spread among mediums.

In 1886 a frail and bespectacled young man named S. J. Davy came to see Hodgson. Davy had been interested in spiritualism and had been particularly taken by some exhibitions of slate writing. During one seance the spirits indicated that Davy himself possessed psychic powers. Later messages appeared mysteriously on a slate that Davy had carried into the seance. Only some weeks after this seance did the young man learn that he had been the victim of a practical joke. He was badly stung, and having plenty of leisure time, he worked on mastering various methods by which slate writing could be produced fraudulently.

With Hodgson's aid he perfected his technique, and then he was introduced to the spiritualist world as an amateur medium. In a series of seances he was able to reproduce virtually all of the methods of slate writing employed by other mediums, and he was never detected in trickery. Ultimately, Davy and Hodgson collaborated on series of articles that not only exposed the trickery involved in the practice of slate writing but also showed great insight into how easily people can be fooled.

This project, naturally, did not endear Richard Hodgson to the spiritualists, and they said that Davy himself was a "renegade medium" who produced genuine phenomena but passed them off as trickery. Still, the practice of slate writing went into a decline in spiritualist circles after the Hodgson-Davy exposés.

In addition to the actual experimental work undertaken by the members of the SPR, the organization determined upon a project that attempted to bring some order out of the chaos surrounding the collection of spontaneous cases. This task was carried on primarily by Edmund Gurney, assisted by Frederic Myers and Frank Podmore. The result was two huge volumes called *Phantasms of the Living* published in 1886. According to Gurney, the book was to deal with "all classes of cases where there is reason to suppose that the mind of one human being has affected the mind of another without speech uttered, or word written, or sign made; has affected, that is to say, by other means than through the recognized channels of sense." It was perhaps the first book ever written on the subject of extrasensory perception.

The book covers some of the experimental work of

the SPR, but the bulk of it is taken up with recording and discussing various "spontaneous cases." The following is a fairly typical case taken from *Phantasms of the Living*. The narrator is Ellen M. Greany, said to be "a trusted and valued servant in the family of Miss Porter."

May 20th, 1884

"I sat one evening reading, when on looking up from my book I distinctly saw a school-friend of mine, to whom I was very much attached standing near the door. I was about to exclaim at the strangeness of her visit when, to my horror, there were no signs of anyone in the room but my mother. I related what I had seen to her knowing she could not have seen, as she was sitting with her back towards the door, nor did she hear anything unusual, and was greatly amused at my scare, suggesting that I read too much or been dreaming.

"A day or so after this strange event, I had news to say my friend was no more. The strange part was that I did not know she was ill, much less in danger, so could not have felt anxious at the time on her account, but may have been thinking of her; that I cannot testify. Her illness was short, and death very unexpected. Her mother told me she spoke of me not long before she died. . . . She died the same evening and about the same time that I saw her vision, which was the end of October 1874."

Ellen M. Greany

The authors of *Phantasms of the Living* add, "In answer to an inquiry, Ellen Greany adds that this hallucination is the only one she has ever experienced. She told Miss Porter that she went to see her dead friend before the funeral, which accords with her statement that she heard the news of the death very soon after it occurred; and there is no reason to doubt that, at the time when she heard the news, she was able correctly to identify the day of her vision."

The book also included the corroborative testimony of Miss Greany's mother and a description of Gurney's interview with Miss Greany, who impressed him as a "superior and intelligent person."

The members of the SPR had tried to move beyond merely collecting odd stories to discovering whether these stories were accurate by checking, as best they could, other witnesses. While working on the project, Gurney wrote up to fifty or sixty letters a day attempting to locate confirming evidence on various accounts. Along with this project, he and his co-workers conducted a large number of personal interviews. From thousands of cases, the authors chose some seven hundred of various types for inclusion in *Phantasms of the Living*.

The response to the publication of this huge work was as might be expected. Those who were predisposed to believe in psychic phenomena received it warmly, whereas those who tended to disbelieve were harshly critical. The critics pointed out that though none of the seven hundred or so cases, presumably the best available to the researchers, was absolutely conclusive, there was always a margin for error, often a considerable margin. Sometimes there were no confirming witnesses; in other cases the person who had the experience might have received the information by normal sensory means but either forgotten or failed to reveal it. There may have been some deliberate hoaxes. Most often the account of the event was not written down until long after it had occurred. The human memory is very unreliable, and the longer the time that passes, the more unreliable it becomes and the stronger the tendency to unconsciously alter details to make an event seem more wonderful or mysterious than it really was. There was a ten-year gap between the time Ellen Greany had her strange experience and the time she wrote it out for the SPR.

Then there was the possibility of coincidence. Sometimes odd things just happen by chance; there is no need to bring in the psychic or supernatural to account for them. To such criticism the Society for Psychical Research responded, "The conclusion is drawn that coincidences of the type in question are far too numerous to be accounted for as accidents; and the establishment of some cause for them, beyond chance, is the proof of Telepathy."

Collecting the evidence for *Phantasms of the Living* brought up an interesting and important question. There seemed to be many odd and possibly psychic experiences to choose from (though the evidential quality of evidence in the stories varied considerably), but how common were such experiences among the general public? Random collecting of accounts could not answer that question. In 1889 the SPR determined to launch an ambitious project called the "Census of Hallucinations." The aim was to determine the frequency of such possibly extrasensory experiences in the public at large. The census question was this: "Have you ever, when believing yourself to be completely awake, had a vivid impression of seeing or being touched by a living being or inanimate object or of hearing a voice; which impression, so far as you could discover, was not due to any external physical cause?"

The SPR investigators obtained replies from some 17,000 persons. Of these 2,272 said that they had experienced such hallucinations. After examining the testimony and eliminating obvious dreams or delirious states, the investigators reduced the number to 1,684. Still it was impressive, for it seemed to indicate that some 10 percent of the British population had at one time or another had an experience that might be classed as psychic. The SPR census was not conducted by modern polling techniques, so the 10 percent figure is questionable. However, fifty-eight years after the original census, D. J. West, a psychical researcher, asked the same question to a smaller, but more carefully chosen sample. This time 14 percent replied in the affirmative. Whatever hallucinations may be, they are not becoming less common.

The most striking finding of the Census of Hallucinations was that of the reported hallucinations eighty of them seemed to coincide within twelve hours either way with the death of the person who was seen or otherwise sensed in the hallucination. The Census Committee examined these reports carefully and eliminated forty-eight of them for one reason or another; still this left thirty-two cases that to the members of the SPR committee seemed striking and fairly well corroborated.

In their report the SPR committee quoted death statistics to show that the occurrence of a hallucination near the time of death was far, far beyond what might be expected from chance. To the census investigators the conclusion seemed clear; some sort of psychic explanation had to account for the high number of cases where the hallucinations were connected with death. The death hallucination or "crisis apparition" as it is often called today is one of the most dramatic and impressive areas investigated by the psychical researchers.

Skeptics were not bowled over by the high number of hallucinations that seemed to coincide with a death. They pointed out that none of the cases cited was conclusively corroborated, and most were not written down until long after the event had supposedly occurred. The SPR investigators admitted that faulty memory, coincidence, or just plain fraud could account for some of their cases; the skeptics asserted that these factors could just as well account for all of them.

Blackburn, who had claimed to have fooled SPR investigators some years earlier, summed up the skeptics' case in these words:

"I am convinced that this propensity to deceive is more general among 'persons of character' than is supposed. I have known the wife of a bishop, when faced with a discrepancy in time in a story of death in India and the appearance of the wraith [ghost or apparition] in England, to deliberately amend her circumstantial story by many hours to fit the altered circumstances. This touching-up process in the telepathic stories I have met again and again, and I say, with full regard to the weight of words, that among the hundreds of stories I have investigated I have not met one that had not a weak link which should prevent its being scientifically established. Coincidences that at first sight appear good cases of telepathic rapport occur to many of us. I have experienced several, but I should hesitate to present them as perfect evidence."

In addition to collecting evidence and conducting experiments, the members of the SPR attempted to evolve some sort of theory that would explain what all these puzzling psychic phenomena meant. The most ambitious early attempt was made by Frederic Myers in a fat volume entitled *Human Personality and Its Survival of Bodily Death*. The book was, unfortunately, not really completed at the time of Myers' own death in 1901. Another, and more serious problem, however, was Myers' writing style. He was more a poet than a scientist, and one sympathetic critic says that "his prose too often dissolves into a kind of Cosmic chant." For example, Myers wrote:

". . . far hence, beyond Orion and Andromeda, the cosmic process works and shall work for ever through unbegotten souls. And even as it was not in truth the great ghost of Hector only, but the whole nascent race

of Rome, which bore from the Trojan altar the hallow-
ing fire, so it is not one Savior only, but the whole
nascent race of man . . ."

In the end, no one was really sure what Myers was
talking about. Certainly his theory was not the sort
that would impress scientists or engage the attention
of the general public. But Myers was not alone in his
failure. Everyone else who has tried to conceive a
general theory of the psychic has encountered similar
problems, and it is fair to conclude that psychical researchers today are no closer to having a comprehensive theory than they were when Myers wrote his book.

By the beginning of the twentieth century, most of
the important founders of the Society for Psychical
Research had died, but from the time the organization
was founded in 1882, this relatively small group of men
and women had been amazingly active. Only a sum-
mary of the highlights of the SPR's work could be given
in this chapter.

The founders of the SPR had hoped, and believed,
that they would be able to establish the case for
psychic phenomena in a relatively short time, but these
hopes were never realized. While some SPR members
were absolutely convinced that they had found conclusive proof of such things as survival after bodily
death, others were far more cautious, and the work of
the SPR did not win over any significant number of
scientific critics.

Research had been started on a number of fronts,
but as the twentieth century dawned, no one seemed
quite sure where it was going to lead.

The Heyday of Card Tests

As a memorial to psychical researcher Richard Hodgson, who died in 1905, a group of his friends established a fund at Harvard University for the purpose of financing psychical research. A number of similar bequests followed, and during the opening years of the twentieth century Harvard became the center for psychical research in America.

A German-born Harvard psychologist named Hugo Munsterberg produced a devastating exposure of the Italian medium Eusapia Palladino, who had some years earlier been exposed in Britain by Hodgson. During a seance Munsterberg had one of his assistants, dressed in black, crawl under the table and grab Eusapia by the foot just as she was trying to pluck the strings of a "ghostly" guitar with her toes.

Less flamboyantly, but more significantly, a few Harvard professors and graduate students began laboratory experiments with telepathy and allied phenomena. In 1916 Harvard psychologist Leonard Troland began to plan a laboratory for the study of psychic subjects. Troland's objective quoted by Milbourne Christopher was "to insure the accurate determination and reproducibility of experimental conditions, to eliminate the personal equation of the investigator and to obtain quantitative data which shall be clearly amenable to mathematical, statistical treatment."

It was a bold plan, but only a few experiments were attempted and nothing really interesting resulted. Psychical research at Harvard picked up in 1920 after the British psychologist William McDougall was appointed to the faculty. At the time of his appointment McDougall was the president of the Society for Psychical Research in Britain. He became president of the American branch of the society shortly after he came to Harvard.

McDougall's presence, in turn, attracted the attention of Joseph Banks Rhine, who was to become the most important figure in American psychical research during the first half of the twentieth century.

Rhine was born in Juniata County, Pennsylvania, in 1895. After his family moved to Ohio, he met and went to school with his future wife and life-long co-worker, Louisa. Both received doctorates in biology at the University of Chicago, but the world of the microscope and the dissecting table held little real fascination for the Rhines.

Both had come from religious backgrounds. Rhine himself had once considered becoming a Protestant minister, but like the British psychical researchers before him, he found that science had pushed him into a position of reluctant skepticism regarding his religion. Yet he was an optimistic man and continued to hope that ultimately the scientific method would be the tool for revealing the true spiritual nature of man.

The Rhines attended a lecture on spiritualism given by Sir Arthur Conan Doyle, author of the Sherlock Holmes stories. Ironically, Doyle, who had created the undeceivable Holmes, was himself the most credulous of men. He accepted practically everything about spiritualism, and his enthusiasm for several notorious frauds embarrassed his more cautious spiritualistic friends. Still he was an impressive figure and a fine lecturer. He was probably the most persuasive propagandist spiritualism has ever had. The Rhines were deeply moved, though they did not accept all or even most of what Doyle had to say about spiritualism. But what if there was some truth in spiritualism? "This mere possibility," Rhine wrote later, "was the most exhilarating thought I had had in years."

There followed a long string of disappointing seances with a variety of mediums. The most notable of these was Margery, wife of a respected Boston surgeon. Margery had captivated some of America's leading psychical researchers before she was conclusively exposed by the great magician Harry Houdini as an arrogant fraud. The Rhines themselves were never deceived; after a single session they concluded that Margery had practiced "brazen trickery."

Rhine wanted to put his scientific training at the

service of psychical research, so he wrote to McDougall and was invited to join him at Harvard. During the year J. B. and Louisa Rhine spent at Harvard, they became closely associated with Dr. Walter Franklin Prince, of the Society for Psychical Research. Mc-Dougall then transferred to Duke University in Durham, North Carolina, where he was to establish a department of psychology. But he retained his interest in psychic phenomena, and when the Rhines followed him to Duke in 1927, he encouraged them to devise laboratory experiments in what came to be called parapsychology. Ultimately, Rhine became head of a separate parapsychology laboratory at Duke.

Oddly, Rhine's first published work concerned the apparent telepathic abilities of a horse named Lady that had been found in Richmond, Virginia. The horse seemed to be able to answer questions by pushing number and letter blocks with her nose. Lady was no real novelty. Counting horses, dogs, and other animals had long been a feature of carnival circuits. The animals, in reality, answered no questions; they merely pushed blocks in response to signals given by their trainers. Often these signals were quite subtle and went unnoticed by onlookers. Rhine should have been more careful, but he endorsed the animal's telepathic abilities in an article published in the *Journal of Abnormal and Social Psychology* in 1929. Later he rather ruefully admitted that in subsequent investigations it was found that the owner of the mare had resorted to signals on some occasions.

At first Rhine was no more successful with people than he had been with horses. He turned away from the psychical researcher's traditional reliance on professional sensitives and started testing ordinary people. A generation of psychical researchers had learned, to their sorrow, that professionals and semiprofessionals were dangerously untrustworthy. Rhine was convinced that everybody possessed ESP abilities to some degree and that it was necessary to locate those whose abilities were more highly developed but who might not know it.

In 1930 Rhine tested a group of youngsters at a summer camp. He asked them to write down a number from 0 to 9 while he stared at a specific number on a numbered card. In approximately one thousand trials no one scored high enough to warrant further investigation. In the fall of 1930 Rhine tested Duke undergraduates, having them guess even letters of the alphabet, numbers, or cards with symbols on them. A total of 1,600 trials again produced only chance results.

The cards with symbols deserve a moment's attention, for Rhine was to use them with increasing success over the next few years, and today the symbols are almost synonymous with the study of ESP. These cards, now called ESP cards, were originally called Zener cards, after K. E. Zener, an early associate of Rhine, who suggested the symbols. The five boldly printed symbols on the face of the cards are a star, a circle, a plus sign, three wavy lines, and a square. Usually five sets of the five symbols, a total of twenty-five cards, make up a deck. These particular symbols were chosen because they were clear and easy to visualize.

There are many ways in which ESP cards can be used. In the standard test for clairvoyance, the pack is shuffled and cut and placed face downward. The subject then attempts to guess the first card, which is removed and placed in a separate pile. He then attempts to guess the second card, and so on through the pack. Only after a complete run-through of the pack are the cards turned over and compared with the guesses. In a variation to test telepathy, a person called the agent looks at the card and tries telepathically to communicate the symbol to a second individual, the percipient.

By pure chance one would expect that a single run-through of the deck in any sort of test would produce five hits or correct guesses out of the twenty-five chances. Of course, not every run will produce a perfect chance result, even if chance is the only factor involved. Sometimes there will be seven or eight hits, and sometimes only three or four. But over an extended series of runs, the pure chance result should average out to five hits out of twenty-five guesses. If someone consistently scored above chance, making six or seven hits per run, this would be considered statistically significant and, in Rhine's view, evidence of ESP. He was not looking for the perfect subject who could guess every card every time, though for a while it appeared as if he had very nearly found some.

Whereas in 1930 experimental progress was slow, it picked up enormously by the end of 1932. Half of the graduate students in psychology at Duke showed some ESP ability. The other half simply had not been tested.

The tests on high-scoring subjects were carried out under a variety of conditions, ranging from very strict to quite informal. One of Rhine's best early subjects was Adam J. Linzmayer. Just as the findings were becoming exciting, Linzmayer had to leave for his summer job. Rhine hoped to conduct a quick series of intensive tests before this prize subject got away, but he had already observed that Linzmayer did not perform well under pressure.

In order to create an informal test situation, Rhine took Linzmayer for a ride in his car and after a while pulled over to the side of the road. With the motor still running, he began a card test. The two men were sitting in the front seat of the car, Rhine behind the wheel and Linzmayer beside him leaning back and shading his eyes with his hand. Rhine shuffled the cards and tilted the top card back far enough so that he could see the symbol, but Linzmayer could not. He then laid the card on a large record book on Linzmayer's lap. Linzmayer made his guess, and Rhine immediately told him whether he was right or wrong. The correct guesses were placed in one pile, the incorrect in another. Linzmayer made fifteen hits in a row and scored another six before that epic run was finished. The odds against such a run occurring by chance, according to Rhine, were 30 billion to one.

Another high-scoring subject was Charles E. Stuart. While Stuart performed fairly well under controlled conditions, he gave his best performance when he tested himself. In a total of 7,500 trials he obtained 1,815 hits against 1,500 hits to be expected by chance.

The case of George Zirkle, another high scorer, was a little more complicated. He did not perform particularly well unless he was working with his fiancée Sara Owenby. In one series of telepathy tests, Miss Owenby and Zirkle sat two rooms apart. When she was ready to concentrate on a card, she pressed a telegraphic key, which signaled Zirkle to record his guess. His performance under these conditions was even more astounding than Linzmayer's, for he correctly identified 23 of a possible 25, 85 of a possible 100, and averaged 16 hits for each run of 25 over 250 trials.

Rhine was naturally elated over such results, but when he published his findings, the critics were savage. They contended that Linzmayer's fantastic performance in the car could have been the result of peeking, or Rhine might have involuntarily tipped off his subject by sensory clues, for example unconsciously whispering the name of the symbol when he looked at the card. The unwitnessed runs were cast aside as utterly worthless.

The Zirkle-Owenby series, however, was not so easily explained away. It took professional magicians to figure out a method by which the high scores could have been obtained by trickery. Milbourne Christopher, the magician, explained: "First, two people practice counting silently until their counts are in unison. Then they give the five symbols numerical values, for example, plus sign—two, wavy lines—three, and square—four. At the start of the test the receiver writes any symbol that comes to his mind for the first entry, but the moment the sending key is pressed both sender and receiver begin counting silently. If the next card is a plus sign, the sender presses the telegraphic key after counting two, if a square after counting four. As sender and receiver are silently counting at the same pace, the receiver gets the second and the next twenty-three cards on cue, and should he make a lucky guess on the first card, he can score a perfect result. Without the lucky guess, a 24 out of 25 is possible, though wise deceptionists would play it cozy and not strain credulity by calling so many correctly."

Other grave shortcomings in Rhine's tests were pointed out particularly regarding the ESP cards themselves. Some of the early cards were printed so heavily that the symbols showed through on the back, and it was possible for someone to know what was on the face of a card by observing the faint impression on its back. In other decks the pattern of the symbol extended to the edges so that it was possible to determine the identity of at least some of the cards in the pack by inspecting the sides of the pack. The cards were often crudely cut, so that when shuffled they tended to fall into a particular pattern rather than in a truly random fashion.

Rhine was strongly disinclined to believe that his

test subjects had been cheating. He also defended the precautions he had taken to guard against cheating and honest error. Rhine said that the critics were simply trying to explain away results that they did not like or did not understand. However, he did acknowledge that some of the early procedures could be tightened up, and he then produced a series of experiments that seemed absolutely conclusive.

The subject in these tests was Hubert E. Pearce, Jr., a divinity student at Duke's School of Religion. Pearce had attended one of Rhine's lectures and then approached him with tales of the psychic abilities in his family. During one table tipping session, Pearce said, his mother had set the table in motion so violently it took two strong men to hold it down.

In 1932 Pearce was tested by Rhine's assistant J. Gaither Pratt, then a graduate student at Duke. The first tests were conducted informally in Pearce's dormitory room, and as he seemed to score above chance with considerable regularity, he was deemed a good subject for more extensive tests.

The most famous of these tests began in the fall of 1933. It was labeled by Rhine the Campus Distance Series but is better known to parapsychologists as the Pearce-Pratt series. These tests were designed to measure clairvoyance over a distance of about a hundred yards. Pratt had an office in the old physics building and Pearce a study cubicle in the library stacks, about a hundred yards away. Some years later Pratt described the conditions of the experiment in his book *Parapsychology*:

"Each day when we planned to work, Hubert would come by my room shortly before the time agreed upon for the test. We compared our watches and set them together, even allowing for the difference between the second hands. Then I watched Hubert walk across the campus and disappear into the library.

"I selected a pack of ESP cards, shuffled it thoroughly, cut it, and placed it face down on the near right-hand corner of a card table at which I had taken my seat. At the time agreed upon for starting the test, I picked up the top card from the pack and, without looking at it, placed it face down on a book in the center of the table. After one minute I removed that card and placed it, still face down and still unknown to myself, at the far left-hand corner of the table and immediately placed the next card from the pack on the book.

"Proceeding in this way, I placed the twenty-five cards, one after the other, on the book, leaving each one there for a minute. Meanwhile Hubert, at his study table in the library, wrote his call for each card sometime during the minute it was on the book in the center of the table. When all the cards had taken their turn on the book, I made a record of the twenty-five cards in the order in which they had been used."

The records of each day's proceedings were placed in sealed envelopes and turned over to Dr. Rhine directly. Pearce and Pratt kept copies of their records and often compared notes later in the day. Over the course of the experiment Pearce scored at better than double chance levels. Pratt said, "You may still choose the chance explanation if you insist, but you would have less than 1 chance in 100,000,000,000,000 of being right! Since it is not reasonable to invoke the chance explanation against such heavy odds, we are bound to find some other interpretation. The conditions appear to leave ESP as the only possibility."

Pearce was tested at other distances, and under other conditions, but his scores became erratic. On some runs he scored very low—too low, thought Pratt, to be easily written off as mere coincidence. He believed that some sort of negative ESP was in operation. At other times Pearce got scores as good as in the original Pearce-Pratt series.

Shortly thereafter Hubert Pearce seemed to lose his ESP ability entirely. He came into the Parapsychology Laboratory one day and said that he had received a letter containing very disturbing news from home. From then on he scored only at chance levels. From time to time in the years since he left Duke to take up a position of Methodist minister in his home state of Kansas, Rhine and Pratt have visited him and conducted card tests, but, alas, with no notable success.

The Pearce-Pratt series seemed to overcome all the objections that had been raised against the previous tests. Unless one assumed that Pearce, Pratt, and Rhine were in collusion to hoodwink the public, fraud seemed to have been ruled out.

The tests intrigued and puzzled Mark Hansel, a psychologist then at the University of Manchester in England and the world's most active academic critic of extrasensory perception research. In 1960 Hansel visited Duke on a grant generously provided by Dr. Rhine. One of Hansel's purposes was to reexamine the physical setting in which the famous series had taken place. Hansel found that the various published reports describing the experiment were inadequate. Pratt and other members of the Parapsychology Laboratory staff were eagerly cooperative. They showed Hansel the office in which Pratt had been seated during the tests, though the office itself had been considerably remodeled in the nearly thirty years since the tests had taken place. No one was able to remember which library cubicle Pearce had occupied. One interesting fact that emerged was that Pearce was not watched while he was supposed to be writing down his calls in the library cubicle. What would have prevented Pearce from leaving the cubicle, sneaking up to Pratt's office, and somehow getting a look at the cards as Pratt was recording their order?

Hansel asked W. Saleh, a member of the research staff at Duke, to run through a pack of ESP cards under conditions that roughly approximated the Pearce-Pratt experiment. Hansel himself, playing the part of Pearce, sat in an office down the corridor from the one in which Saleh ran through the pack of cards. During the experiment Hansel walked down to Saleh's room and by standing on a chair he could look through a crack at the top of the door and view the cards as Saleh was recording them. When Hansel turned in his score, he had 22 hits out of 25, and Saleh had no idea of what had happened.

Hansel then tried another trick. He left a sheet of

blotting paper on the desk on which Saleh was to record the cards during another test. The blotting paper was to take an impression of what he wrote, and Hansel was able to read off the identities of the cards from impressions on the blotting paper. "But by this time Saleh was tired of having his leg pulled," Hansel wrote in *ESP: A Scientific Evaluation.* "He had carefully written out a second list, using the blotting paper for it, so that I was given false information. It was clear, however, from these tests that knowledge of the cards could have been obtained by the use of either method, provided the other factors in the situation did not eliminate the possibility."

Hansel has himself been sharply criticized by parapsychologists. They say that his reconstruction of the original Pearce-Pratt series in no way matches the conditions of the test and is therefore invalid. Hansel's reply has been that since no one can really remember the original conditions, the series has to be regarded as less than conclusive, for the possibility of fraud had not been completely ruled out. "Rhine might well have been wary of trickery," he wrote, "for neither he nor Pratt were novices in psychical research. Both of them were fully aware of its long history of trickery."

One of Rhine's most prickly critics during the early days of his research was a British mathematician named S. G. Soal. According to Mark Hansel, Soal, in an outburst of nationalistic pique, asserted that the "marvels" Rhine had discovered would in Britain be "quickly exposed as frauds or conjuring tricks," but that in America "they are proclaimed as genuine with a blare of trumpets."

Soal, however, was no skeptic about the existence of ESP and had been deeply involved in psychical research since the 1920s. By 1939 the mathematician had conducted well over 100,000 card guessing trials with 140 different individuals, but found no evidence of ESP abilities among his subjects. Instead of the familiar American ESP cards, Soal used animal cards of his own design. On the face of these cards were five different animal symbols: a penguin, an elephant, a giraffe, a zebra, and a lion.

In 1939 Soal was persuaded to reexamine his extensive test records to see whether any of the subjects were scoring, not on the target card, but on the card one ahead or one behind the target. With this reexamination Soal found two subjects, Mrs. Gloria Stewart and Basil Shackleton, who seemed to display some sort of above-chance ability.

Mrs. Stewart had been introduced to Soal in 1936. Shackleton, a professional photographer, had contacted Soal the same year after reading of his experiments in the newspapers. Shackleton said that he possessed psychic abilities and had not come to test them, but to display them.

Over three years after he first tested Shackleton, Soal began exhaustively retesting him. The retests themselves took several years. Soal was testing Shackleton in 1941 during the height of the German blitz of London. They sat in Shackleton's studio calmly turning over cards and recording guesses while German bombs fell around them.

The photographer's ESP ability seemed unaffected by the stressful times. He made 1,101 correct guesses out of a run of 3,789 cards. The odds against such a run occurring by chance are astronomical. However, Shackleton was not guessing on target. Just as he had done previously, he was correctly guessing the next card to come up. When the test was speeded up, Shackleton's correct guesses jumped two cards ahead. This time he scored 236 hits out of 794 trials.

While most of the tests were held in Shackleton's studio, a few were held in the offices of the SPR. Controls for the tests varied. Sometimes Shackleton sat in one room while the experimenter sat in another turning over the cards; at other times Shackleton and the experimenter sat on opposite sides of a table with a large screen between them. During some of the tests, outsiders were brought in as observers. Later, Mark Hansel tells us, Soal wrote that no "ultra-rigorous precautions on fraud" were carried out "on the part of the experimenters" because if they are "not to be trusted, there is no point whatever in doing the experiments." At another time he wrote, "But it never entered my mind that Mrs. Stewart or Mr. Shackleton would try consciously to cheat, they are not the sort of people who cheat."

Critics of ESP research were not reassured by these statements. Still they found Soal's precautions against cheating reasonably adequate. There seemed no obvious way in which Shackleton or Mrs. Stewart, who was retested after the second Shackleton series was completed, could have cheated without the aid of Soal himself or someone else closely connected with the experiment. With two or more people "in on the trick," cheating would have been fairly easy, for the records could have been altered. There is, however, no solid information to indicate that such a "conspiracy" ever took place. Soal's experiments with Shackleton and Mrs. Stewart remain the best of the card-guessing tests in the opinion of most parapsychologists.

Soal continued his experiments, and in 1955 he discovered two more high-scoring subjects. They were Glyn and Ieuan Jones, a pair of thirteen-year-old schoolboys who lived in the small village of Capel Curig in North Wales. When tested in their home, the boys apparently displayed remarkable telepathic abilities. Though the controls on the tests were not very tight, the boys seemed to be worth more extensive examination. They were brought to the offices of the SPR in London, and there they continued their high-scoring ways.

Observers, however, noticed some strange things about these tests. The boys did a lot of shifting about in their chairs, coughing, and sneezing. Soal's co-worker, Mrs. K. M. Goldney of the SPR, found that Ieuan's chair creaked three times whenever he concentrated on a lion card, and that when it did, his brother guessed the card correctly. It was the same sort of crude code that the Creery sisters had used to fool members of the SPR more than a half century earlier.

The boys had a good reason for trying to get high scores because Soal paid them for every correct call that they made. On a good run they could make a considerable amount of money, particularly for poor Welsh schoolboys. Soal believed that the payment plan provided a strong incentive for the boys to concentrate on the tests—but it also provided a strong incentive to cheat. Finally the boys did admit cheating on some occasions, but promised that they would never do it again, so Soal resumed his tests.

One series of tests conducted on the Jones boys was supervised by Jack Salvin, a professional magician and an expert on mind-reading tricks. Salvin and his wife had once performed a mind-reading act in which they had used various sorts of signals. According to Milbourne Christopher, Salvin gave the boys a clean bill of health. "Code or trickery in the experimental conditions I witnessed is impossible."

No tricks should have escaped the notice of an observer of Salvin's experience. Yet, Mark Hansel, who had investigated the tests, believed that the magician had overlooked one possibility. Salvin was a man in his seventies, whereas the boys were young teen-agers. The sense that deteriorates most markedly with age is hearing. Hansel theorized that the boys might have used a silent dog whistle as a signal. These devices have such a high pitch that they are out of the range of hearing of most adults, but they are easily heard by dogs and often can be detected by youngsters with good hearing. In order for Hansel's trick to work, the boys would have to have had an accomplice in the room to do the actual signaling. In most of the tests a relative, usually the boys' father, was present as an observer and could have served as an accomplice.

Hansel tested his theory on several people in their forties, and none were able to detect the dog whistle. Hansel attached the whistle to a piece of rubber tubing with a rubber ball on the end. This he concealed in his pocket, and he could "blow" the whistle simply by squeezing the ball. Salvin himself was later fooled during tests where the receiver and sender were cuing one another with a concealed dog whistle. He admitted frankly that during this session he had detected no evidence of deception. Nevertheless, there was no proof that such a whistle had been used in the tests on Glyn and Ieuan Jones.

Like Pearce, Shackleton, and all the other high-scoring subjects of the past, the Jones boys seemed to lose their telepathic powers, and in April of 1957, Soal decided to abandon testing them. Since that time neither Soal nor Rhine has been able to locate any consistently high-scoring subjects, and it seems that, at least for the moment, the heyday of card-guessing tests is over.

It would, of course, be possible to construct card-guessing tests that are absolutely fraud-proof. But Rhine has argued that rigid and mechanistic controls disrupt the subtle ESP effect. "Elaborate precautions take their toll," he has said. "Experimenters who have worked long in this field have observed that the scoring rate is hampered as the experiment is made complicated, heavy, and slow-moving. Precautionary measures are usually distracting in themselves." Some parapsychologists insist that the reason no more consistently high-scoring subjects have been found is that today's controls are too rigid. Skeptics, on the other hand, say that the controls have simply eliminated the possibility of fraud and error, and without fraud and error there is no ESP.

By the end of the 1950s, Rhine and Soal found themselves in a position similar to that of the founders of the SPR at the beginning of the 1900s. Research in extrasensory perception had been made increasingly respectable, and both men were convinced that their tests had adequately proved ESP—and yet the doubts persisted. The final and conclusive experiment had not yet been performed.

5

The Current Scene

If the symbol of research into extrasensory perception during the 1930s and 40s was the ESP card, the symbol of one branch of ESP research today would be the machine—or rather a variety of different kinds of machines. Parapsychologists are trying to use new technology to pin down the elusive extrasensory phenomena.

Possibly the most important machine introduced into ESP research is the electroencephalograph (EEG), which can measure weak electrical impulses emanating from the human body. The impulses are picked up by tiny electrodes that are attached to the subject's head or body. Wires from the electrodes carry the impulses to the EEG console itself, where they are "translated" into wavy lines scratched out by pens on a piece of moving graph paper. An experienced EEG operator can "read" the lines and know just what is happening in the subject's body at that moment.

Use of the EEG in parapsychology research is not itself a new development. The machine was invented in 1929 by Hans Berger, who believed that it could be used to measure the energy responsible for extrasensory perception. This did not work out as Berger had hoped, but the EEG has proved very useful in other ways.

In the 1950s the EEG became a primary tool for research into sleeping and dreaming. Scientists found that during a normal night there were different stages of sleep and that these could be determined by electrical impulses emanating from the brain. They also found that everybody has several dreams every night. When a sleeper is dreaming, his eyes move rapidly back and forth under his closed lids. It is almost as if the sleeper were following the action of the dream with his eyes.

We usually forget our dreams by the time we awaken. For that reason many people believe that they never dream, or dream very rarely. Even if a dream is recalled, memory of it is poor and partial, and details are often filled in by the conscious mind, thus altering the dream. If the sleeper is awakened in the middle of a dream, then his recall is much better, but there is no way of telling when a sleeper is dreaming just by looking at him. However, when electrodes are taped near a sleeping subject's eyes, the energy put out during periods of rapid eye motion (REM) is easily detectable by the EEG. The EEG operator can thus tell just exactly when a subject is dreaming. This discovery opened an entirely new field of research in sleep and dreams.

The discovery also opened a new field of research for parapsychology. Dreams had long been a rich source of stories of spontaneous extrasensory experiences. Since ancient times prophetic dreams had been highly regarded. Modern parapsychologists often speculated that during sleep when the conscious mind was not active, the unconscious mind became more receptive to extrasensory impressions. With the use of the EEG, it seemed possible to move this potentially valuable field of investigation from the mere collecting of half-remembered dreams that seemed to be extrasensory into an organized laboratory study of the ESP content of dreams.

Laboratories to study sleep and dreaming were established at a number of universities and medical centers throughout the country. Most of those engaged in sleep and dream research either did not believe in ESP or were simply uninterested in looking for it. In the dream laboratory of Maimonides Hospital in Brooklyn, however, researchers have been looking specifically for evidence of extrasensory perception since the lab was first established in 1964. The experiments in the Maimonidies dream laboratory are under the supervision of Dr. Stanley Krippner, director of the lab, and Dr. Montague Ullman, head of the psychiatry department at Maimonides, and also president of the American Society for Psychical Research. Over the years Drs. Krippner and Ullman believe that their tests have produced a mass of evidence that overwhelmingly supports the ESP hypothesis.

Work at the Maimonides dream lab began with relatively simple telepathy tests. The sleeper, generally someone the lab staff felt had demonstrated extrasensory ability, would retire for the night into a soundproof bedroom, with a batch of electrodes taped firmly to his or her head. Wires from the electrodes led to an EEG machine in an adjoining room. There one of the lab staff watched as seven pens scratched out red wavy lines on a moving sheet of graph paper. The lines were measurements of seven different types of energy from the sleeping subject.

In a third room, often one at the other end of the building, sat the agent or sender. It was his job to concentrate on a picture, usually a photograph of a painting chosen at random from the lab's large collection. The agent was to attempt to "send" a mental image of this target picture to the sleeping subject.

After a strong pattern of REMs appeared to indicate that the subject was dreaming, he was awakened by a buzzer, and the experimenter asked him what he had been dreaming about. His description of the dream was recorded on tape. The subject then went back to sleep. This routine could be repeated four or five times during the night, depending on how many dreams the subject had.

In the morning there was a "dream review," where the subject was once again asked to retell his dreams and describe what the dreams made him think of. The subject was then shown twelve pictures, including the target picture, and asked which one matched his dreams most closely. The procedure would be repeated on succeeding nights with different subjects and different paintings. At the end of a run of twelve subjects, transcripts of what they had said about their dreams and prints of the target paintings were submitted to three independent judges who were to evaluate the telepathic content of the dreams.

The most striking "hit" according to dream lab staff members was with Van Gogh's *Boats on the Beach* as the target painting. In describing his dream, the subject spoke of "being on a boardwalk or a beach . . . the seacoast. The place is slightly elevated . . . it makes me think of Van Gogh."

A painting called *Animals* by Tamayo, showing hungry dogs standing over some bones and a huge black rock in the background, brought about this dream description from a subject: "I was eating something like rib steak. And this friend of mine was there. People were talking about how she wasn't very good to invite to dinner because she was very conscious of other people getting more to eat than she got, especially meat." The subject also used the words "black rock" several times and spoke of "that mermaid from the Black Rock bar . . . "

A cab driver had as his target picture George Bellows' painting of a famous boxing match, *Dempsey and Firpo*. During his report he mentioned persistent images that seemed related to boxing: "Something about posts," he recalled. "There's a feeling of moving. Ah, something about Madison Square Garden and a boxing match." Later the same night he dreamed about "a square shape . . . two or three figures . . . and the presence of other people."

In 1968 a writer reported an impression of a martyred death from several dreams. "I was hearing the chorus, 'Give them the ax, give them the ax,' from *The Boys from Syracuse*," he said. The target painting was Burne-Jones' *Perseus and the Graces*, in which the hero Perseus is shown with the Three Graces shortly before he beheads the Medusa.

When Gauguin's *The Moon and the Earth*, a painting showing a naked dark-skinned girl by a stream of water, was target, a secretary reported dreaming of "scantily clad girls." She pictured herself in a bathing suit, and in one dream she saw "a dancing girl" with "dark tan shoulders."

Though they seem striking, these dream lab tests lack the unambiguous clarity of the classic card-guessing tests. Though occasionally it appears that a few words from the dream description relate perfectly to the target picture, this sort of "hit" is often less impressive when one reads through an entire transcript. The subjects ramble on about many things while describing their dreams, and the amount that relates to the target painting may be only a tiny part of the total description. For many subjects there seems no relationship at all between the dream and the target painting. The significance, or lack of it, in such tests cannot be measured by coldly impersonal statistics; it is always a matter of human and thus fallible interpretation.

In this drawing showing biblical figures in sixteenth-century dress, the Hebrew prisoner Joseph is called before Pharaoh to interpret the ruler's dream. *(New York Public Library: Picture Collection)*

St. Joseph of Copertino, a seventeenth-century monk, was said to levitate and even to fly. *(New York Public Library: Picture Collection)*

RIGHT: Henry Sidgwick, an early investigator of spiritualism in England, served as the first president of the Society for Psychical Research. *(Society for Psychical Research)*

BELOW: At a seance, medium Jack Webber supposedly caused a forty-five-pound table to levitate while he was tied to his chair. *(Society for Psychical Research)*

LEFT: Joseph Banks Rhine, a pioneer in the use of card tests for ESP, dominated American psychical research in the first half of the twentieth century. *(Wide World Photos)*

OPPOSITE PAGE RIGHT: In this simple card-guessing experiment, the agent, at the left, turns up cards and tries to fix the symbol in her mind while the percipient records her guess on a score sheet. *(John H. Cutten)*

BELOW: Two types of cards used in ESP tests are shown here: animal cards, designed by S. G. Soal, and those with symbols, used by J. B. Rhine. *(Society for Psychical Research)*

BELOW LEFT: At the Maimonides Dream Laboratory, an experiment to find a relationship between extrasensory impressions and dreams begins with a subject having electrodes taped to her head and attached to an EEG machine. (*Harold Friedman*)   BELOW RIGHT: Later, the agent in the telepathy experiment studies a reproduction of a painting and tries to transmit her thoughts about it to the sleeping subject. (*Harold Friedman*)

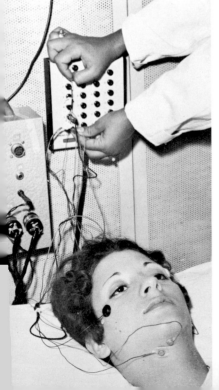

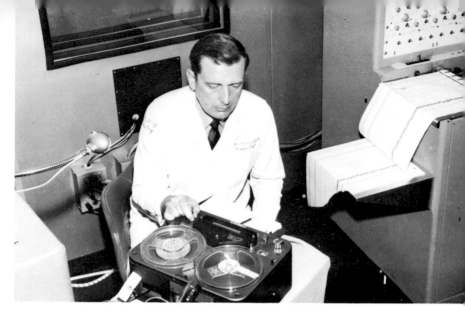

ABOVE: During the night, the subject's descriptions of her dreams are taped by Dr. Stanley Krippner. *(Harold Friedman)*   BELOW: The following morning the subject tries to pick the painting that most closely matches her dream while a staff member of the dream laboratory records her responses. *(Harold Friedman)*

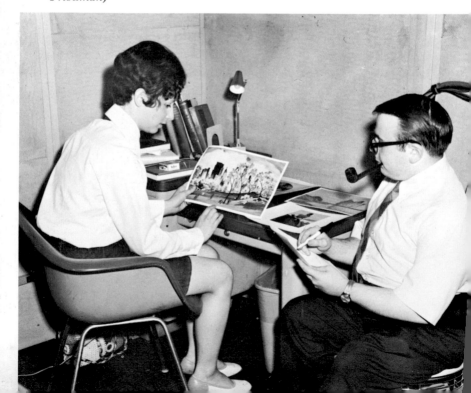

ABOVE: One of the earliest spirit photographs shows a man named Charles Foster being embraced by a shadowy figure. *(Society for Psychical Research)*

BELOW: Dutch psychic Gerard Croiset has become well known for his alleged abilities in solving crimes. *(ABC Television Network)*

This electronically triggered photographic apparatus, described by its designer John Cutten as a "ghost detection device," is set off by the types of disturbances often reported by people as evidence of a poltergeist—wind, noise, change in lighting, vibration, or pressure on a trip wire. Mr. Cutten has said of his invention, "I do not expect this to photograph a ghost. If it got a picture of the cat knocking something over in the night, for instance, it would have served its purpose by showing what did cause the disturbance." *(John H. Cutten)*

One oddity turned up by dream lab research is that the subjects themselves often had considerable difficulty linking their dreams with the target paintings, though outside judges were able to see a correlation at once. In a 1968 study, subjects linked their dreams and target paintings in only 64 percent of the cases, a figure that dream lab researchers said was not quite statistically significant. Judges, on the other hand, linked written reports of the same dreams with targets in 91 percent of the cases—definitely a statistically significant figure.

Dr. Krippner suggests that the disparity may be due to the fact that subjects have no chance to study their dream reports before they choose a target. They may simply have forgotten details of their dreams, just as the average person does when he wakes up.

The experimenters could, of course, have used ordinary ESP cards as targets. This would have avoided some of the confusion and ambiguity involved in attempting to work out a correlation with a target as complicated as a painting. But one of the major criticisms of the card-guessing tests is that they are too sterile and devoid of emotional content. The clear and simple symbols fail to engage the emotions or even the interest of the subject. ESP researchers have long held that extrasensory perception is somehow connected both with emotions and interest level. Paintings, the Maimonides researchers believe, offer a more emotional content, and that more than compensates for the less than statistically perfect results.

In fact, in recent years dream researchers have tried many methods for reinforcing the target picture. In later experiments the picture was accompanied by scents, music, or objects that related to it. These were presented to the agent along with the picture itself.

When the target picture was *Downpour at Shono* by Hiroshige, which showed a Japanese man with an umbrella trying to escape from a driving rain, it was accompanied by a toy Japanese umbrella. During the session the dreamer reported images of fountains and rain.

In a later test with the same subject, the target picture was Max Beckmann's *The Descent from the Cross,* showing an emaciated Jesus being taken down from the cross. To reinforce this picture, the experimenters used a crucifix, a picture of Jesus, and several thumbtacks. In describing his dreams, the subject spoke of ritual sacrifice, an emaciated figure (described as a debilitated Winston Churchill, who in reality was quite heavy), and the idea of a god who spoke through the sacrificial victims. Images of wine and cannibalism also appeared in the dream.

These tests, however, were simple when compared to a series of precognition tests conducted in the dream laboratory in 1969 with a young British sensitive, Malcolm Bessent. Instead of just using a picture, Dr. Krippner tried to create what he calls a "multisensory environment" in order to give the psychic's ESP something with more emotional content to work on. Malcolm went to sleep and recorded his dreams in the usual way. However, there was no agent looking at a target picture and trying to "send it" to the sleeper; in fact, there was no target picture—yet. The objective of the test was to see if Malcolm could dream about a picture that had not yet been chosen.

The contents of Malcolm's dreams were known only to the member of the lab staff actually monitoring the EEG machine. The following morning other members of the lab staff, who had no idea what Malcolm had dreamed about, went through the process of choosing a target picture.

First the staff members would choose a number from a table of random numbers. This number would in turn lead them to a specific page and one of 12,000 key words in a book of dream descriptions. This word would then be given to Dr. Krippner. He would try to find a painting in the lab's large collection that related to the target word.

Here is how the experiment went in practice. Remember now that the aim of the test was to discover whether Malcolm had precognition—whether he could see the future. Thus, the usual order of an extrasensory perception test was reversed. First came the dream, and only afterward was the target picked.

Herbert Greenhouse in his book *Premonitions: A Leap into the Future* tells us that on the first night of a series of tests, Malcolm reported his dream. "I saw a large concrete building . . . a patient escaping from upstairs . . . she had a white coat on, like a doctor's coat, and people were arguing with her in the street . . . medical people . . . white cups on a tray . . ."

In his dream review upon awakening in the morning,

Malcolm once again talked of the large concrete build-ing, doctors, psychologists, a mental patient escaping from a hospital, and a feeling of hostility.

All of this was unknown to the lab workers when they chose the target word for the experiment. It turned out to be *corridor*. To fit this word Dr. Krippner picked the Van Gogh painting *Corridor of the St. Paul Hospital*.

In order to create a "multisensory environment," a little drama built around the painting was staged for Malcolm in midmorning after the dream session. He was led away by two grim-looking hospital attendants. They took him through a long dark corridor (the target word) and into a room. In the background a phono-graph played the eerie theme from the psychological movie *Spellbound*, and recorded sounds of hysterical laughter were interspersed with the music. On the wall of the room hung a print of the Van Gogh picture, and behind the desk sat Dr. Krippner himself with a wild look in his eyes. Every so often he would laugh hysterically.

Dr. Krippner addressed Malcolm as "Mr. Van Gogh," ordered him to swallow a pill, and wiped his face with a cotton swab. Weird drawings were flashed on the wall, and Malcolm was told that they were the work of mental patients. By this time Malcolm may well have wondered whether it was not Dr. Krippner himself who had gone mad.

Only after the drama was played out did Dr. Krip-pner learn the content of Malcolm's dreams and

Malcolm learn the target word and picture. The staff at the laboratory felt that Malcolm's dreams gave strong indications that he had foreseen what was going to happen to him the next day. On six succeeding nights similar tests of Malcolm Bessent's abilities seemed to produce equally significant results, or very nearly so.

On the third night Malcolm reported of one of his dreams, "All I can think of is a bowl of fruit." He repeated the words "bowl of fruit" during the morning dream review. The picture that was chosen after the dream was Cokovsky's *Fruits and Flowers*. As part of Dr. Krippner's "multisensory environment," Malcolm was shown a bowl of fruit and asked to smell it and eat some. Again Malcolm seemed to have dreamed about an event before it happened.

The Maimonidies experiments represent one side of the current ESP research scene. Many people in psychical research have become discouraged with the apparent dead-end reached by the Rhine and Soal type of card-guessing tests. They have advocated a return to the more free-wheeling case history approach. Such a return is tempting. It is far more interesting to hear stories of strange events than it is to sit in a laboratory room and tediously record card guesses, but stories have been collected for hundreds of years. Even the founders of psychical research realized that all the stories in the world would not move them any closer to understanding the nature of ESP or to making the skeptical scientific community less skeptical. The laboratory approach could not be abandoned, but Doctors Ullman and Krippner and the staff at the dream laboratory have tried to reintroduce the missing "emotional element" into their studies.

By bringing in the emotional element, however, the dream researchers have opened their experiments to charges that significant results are not due to ESP but to an overgenerous interpretation of what is supposed to be significant. Then, too, there is always the possibility of fraud. Is there no way that some of the subjects of the Maimonidies experiments could have known what the target word would be, or somehow have made sure that a particular target picture would be chosen? The Maimonides experimenters believe that their controls have been more than adequate—yet in the past other psychical researchers have also believed their controls to be adequate, only to discover that they had been deceived. The researchers at the dream laboratory have been reluctant to allow skeptical outsiders to monitor their experiments too closely. Like many psychical researchers they believe that the overbearing presence of skeptics tends to disrupt ESP.

Another modern approach to the study of ESP is to construct experiments that are more rigorous than the classic card tests and thus less open to charges of fraud, error, and mistaken interpretation. In 1963 the Air Force Cambridge Research Laboratories conducted an investigation of ESP in which the whole testing and recording procedure was carried out by machine. The investigators hoped to set up an ESP test that was absolutely foolproof.

The machine used was called VERITAC. It automatically generated random targets—the digits from 0 to 9. The subject sitting at the console of the machine pressed a button to register his guess, and a light flashed if he made the correct guess. Some parapsychologists have found that subjects get better scores if they are kept appraised of how they are doing. The machine also kept a record of the total number of correct guesses and figured up the score at the end of the test.

A group of 37 subjects completed a total of 55,500 trials, and no evidence of any sort of ESP ability was discovered among them, even though some had shown extrasensory abilities in earlier but less rigorous tests. The experimenters, however, asserted that this series of tests was merely preliminary and could in no way be considered evidence that ESP did not exist. They felt they were merely setting up procedures and testing the equipment. Unfortunately, however, this very promising work was never continued.

While the Air Force scientists produced no evidence of ESP with VERITAC, a professional parapsychologist, using an even more elaborate bit of equipment, did come up with what he considered to be significant results. The scientist is Dr. Helmut Schmidt, a physicist who formerly worked for the Boeing Scientific Research Laboratories and who later, after Dr. Rhine retired, became director of the Institute for Parapsychology at Duke University.

On the surface Schmidt's experiments look simple. A subject is asked to guess which of four lamps on a machine will light up next. This might be a test for precognition or for psychokinesis, for the subject might, in some subtle and unexplained way, be influencing the choice of lights. Schmidt was trying to demonstrate the existence of some sort of extrasensory ability—it didn't really matter which one. The complexity of the experiment lies in the way in which the choice of lights is determined. According to Arthur Koestler in his book *The Roots of Coincidence*, Schmidt said that the flashing of the lights was controlled by "a single quantum process, the arrival and registration of an electron (from a radioactive strontium 90 source) at a geiger-Muller tube." This sort of basic physical process should be completely unpredictable, and thus the lamps should be lit in a thoroughly random fashion. There should be no ordinary way of predicting or influencing the lights.

By pure chance the subject should make correct guesses 25 percent of the time. In one series of experiments the average scoring levels were 26.1 percent, in the second 27 percent, and in the third 26.7 percent. Not dramatic results, but statistically significant results if achieved over a long period of trials and if the machine was producing a truly random pattern of lighting.

Schmidt's results were published not only in the regular parapsychology journals, but also in more conservative and orthodox scientific publications. They stirred up a controversy that continues to this day. The basis of the objections to the findings was summed up at a 1970 parapsychology convention by critic Mark Hansel: "I think one has to first consider repeatability. I would like other people to be able to claim the same results, and I would like the actual apparatus to be examined. One would like to know that the apparatus is operating efficiently."

Even parapsychologists who desperately wish to see ESP become an established and respectable branch of scientific study have not been entirely satisfied with Schmidt's "single quantum process." C. W. K. Mundale, a philosopher and president of the British Society for Psychical Research, gave a speech in which he praised Schmidt's techniques to the skies. But in the end he was forced to conclude that "if 26 to 27 percent is the best scoring level that can be achieved with this gadget, the method has one obvious disadvantage— subjects may die of boredom" because such long series are needed to obtain results that would be considered statistically significant.

As Mundale indicated, Schmidt's experiments, while they may be highly significant, are also highly undramatic. In February, 1971, there was an experiment that was not particularly significant, but it had an unparalleled dramatic quality and must be mentioned. An attempt was made to transfer thoughts across a quarter of million miles—from the earth to the moon. Edgar Mitchell, one of the three astronauts on the Apollo 14 moon flight, had been deeply interested in ESP for many years—in fact, since his flight he has become something of an evangelist for psychic phenomena.

Some months before his flight, Mitchell contacted a group of parapsychologists and asked them to pick a sensitive subject, one who might be able to receive his thoughts transmitted from the moon.

The man chosen was Olof Jonsson, a Chicago drafting engineer and a fairly well-known nonprofessional psychic. Jonsson and Mitchell conducted some informal experiments to see if they were in proper rapport. At Cape Kennedy, Florida, Mitchell arranged a deck of standard ESP cards in a particular sequence, and then he tried to transmit the sequence of cards to Jonsson in Chicago a thousand miles away. The results satisfied both men, and they decided to try the same thing over the vastly greater distance from earth to moon. In most past experiments in telepathy the distance between sender and percipient appeared to make no difference, so while the moon-to-earth experiment was spectacular, it did not touch upon the basic problems of ESP research.

The experiment was completely unofficial. Indeed, when news of it came out after the flight, Mitchell was subjected to some fairly heavy criticism for "wasting valuable time" while he was on the moon. Mitchell, however, worked on this project only during his rest periods. In all, he and Jonsson conducted six experiments of six minutes each, one on each of the three days before and after the moon landing. During the six-minute period Mitchell attempted to transfer to earth about twenty-five different images of cards. Both Mitchell and Jonsson kept careful records, which were compared after Mitchell returned to earth. But the Chicago sensitive found that his "receptivity" varied. Sometimes he seemed to be receiving Mitchell's thoughts clearly, but during other periods the picture of the cards was blurred or entirely absent. In the periods in which Jonsson was receiving well, he averaged seven hits out of the twenty-five images. Even if the score was much better than it turned out to be, there were far too few trials for the results to be considered significant or conclusive.

As we said, Astronaut Mitchell's involvement with ESP experiments was strictly unofficial, but there has been a great deal of misunderstanding concerning the official support that the National Aeronautics and Space Administration and other government agencies have given to ESP research. Aside from the short-lived project with VERITAC in 1963, there appears to have been no direct government funding of ESP projects. Some government scientists and technicians are interested in ESP and may have conducted unofficial experiments, as did Astronaut Mitchell. Many may hope rather wistfully that money for a major research project will be forthcoming, but so far this has not happened. However, there have been numerous rumors concerning the "secret" involvement of both the U.S. and Soviet governments in ESP projects. Despite repeated denials by both government officials and respectable parapsychologists, such rumors continue to circulate. They create excitement, but in the end they do not really help the field of parapsychology because they are so baseless that they tend to drive away serious and honest people who might otherwise be interested.

In 1959 there was a rumor that the U.S. atomic submarine *Nautilus* had engaged in highly successful ship-to-shore telepathy experiments that might have military significance. The rumor was started in a story entitled "Thought Transmission—Weapon of War?" that appeared in a generally reliable French popular science magazine. The French magazine refused to reveal its source for this sensational story, as well it might. The story has been flatly denied by absolutely everyone who could have been connected with the alleged experiments. The *Nautilus* itself was in dry dock at Portsmouth, N.H., when the experiments were supposed to have taken place. In short, the experiments could not have taken place, and the story was a hoax.

In the field of parapsychology, however, hoaxes can sometimes have strange results. The French articles came to the attention of a Russian psychologist named Leonid L. Vasiliev. Vasiliev had long been interested in ESP and had conducted some experiments during the 1920s and 30s. However, the Soviet government is officially committed to the doctrine of materialism. Psychical research with its attempt to discover a non-material and spiritual side of nature has never been very popular with Soviet officialdom. Vasiliev himself had attempted to formulate theories that would account for ESP by radiation or some other factor that could be fitted into a materialist theory. His attempt was never very successful, and from 1939 to 1959

Leonid L. Vasiliev and his ESP experiments dropped out of sight. But armed with the French stories, which indicated that the U.S. was finding military significance in ESP research, Vasiliev apparently was able to convince his superiors to allow him to continue ESP research, at least on a small scale.

Thus, it seems that a hoax helped to stimulate modern ESP research in the Soviet Union. The story does not end there either. In 1963 the *Chicago Tribune* printed an article stating that the Russians had eight large ESP laboratories in operation. The story said that they "conducted experiments which, if the results are half as good as the Russians claim, indicate that they may be the first to put a human thought in orbit or achieve mind-to-mind communication with men on the moon." The story, though it was not true, did anticipate Astronaut Mitchell's attempt.

The tale of the eight laboratories, which seems to have been a greatly exaggerated account of the work being done by Vasiliev and a few other Soviet scientists and technicians interested in ESP, was repeated endlessly in the popular press. Professional parapsychologists, who were more aware of what was and was not going on in the Soviet Union, never endorsed such a wild claim and indeed often went out of their way to stress that these stories were unsupported and probably untrue. But tales of a great psychic "breakthrough" in Russia continued to circulate. Some ESP enthusiasts seemed to be trying to create the idea of a "parapsychology gap" between the U.S. and Russia. Perhaps they hoped that this would stimulate psychical research in the same way that the idea of a "missile gap" stimulated aerospace research.

Parts of the original *Chicago Tribune* story were picked up by an important NASA scientist and repeated without credit in a speech he gave to an international astronautics meeting. It appeared that NASA itself was endorsing the tale of the large Soviet ESP labs, though this certainly was not the case. This speech was made in 1966, and a prominent reference to it appears in an influential book on parapsychology that was published in 1972. In the field of parapsychology, once an interesting rumor gets started, it is virtually impossible to kill off.

Once again popular interest in Soviet ESP research is on the rise in the West. This is due primarily to an extremely popular book entitled *Psychic Discoveries Behind the Iron Curtain*. The book was written by Sheila Ostrander and Lynn Schroeder, two Americans who toured the Soviet Union and other Eastern bloc countries, talking to scientists and others interested in psychical research. Though much of the publicity surrounding this book hints that there is a great national effort in the Soviet Union aimed at harnessing extrasensory perception and that scientists there have achieved astonishing results, what emerges is that there are a small number of individuals with some scientific training who are conducting experiments in ESP. Far from making any great breakthroughs, Eastern European ESP research must be considered highly unsophisticated compared to what is going on now in the West.

One of the most sensational cases reported in *Psychic Discoveries Behind the Iron Curtain* concerns a psychic called Nelya Mikhailova (a pseudonym). Mikhailova is most famed for her psychokinetic (PK) ability, that is, her ability to apparently move small objects about through the employment of an unknown psychic force.

Ostrander and Schroeder thoroughly endorsed Mikhailova's PK claims, though they had not seen her in person. No Westerner, particularly no Western parapsychologist, has had a chance to test her. Mikhailova is also far from being universally popular in her native land; indeed, she has regularly been denounced as a fraud and is probably considered as such by the majority of Soviet scientists who consider her at all. Her position is very like that of the mediums of the nineteenth and early twentieth centuries. Ostrander and Schroeder compare Mikhailova to Eusapia Palladino, the Italian medium who made such a splash in the early decades of this century. This comparison may be more accurate than Ostrander and Schroeder intended it to be, for most people with scientific training, as well as most professional magicians and a fair percentage of respectable psychical researchers as well, were convinced that Eusapia was either a complete fraud or that she certainly used fraud to produce her most spectacular effects. On the other hand, Eusapia did have a few prominent and well-respected supporters.

The authors of *Psychic Discoveries Behind the Iron Curtain* viewed a film of Mikhailova in action while they were in Moscow. The film showed Mikhailova sitting at a table upon which a number of small objects —a compass, a wrist band, a cigarette, a pen top, a metal cylinder, and a matchbook—had been placed. With a good deal of apparent effort, consisting of shifting, squirming, and waving her hand about, Mikhailova first caused the compass needle to rotate and then moved some of the other objects. The authors were much impressed by the film.

This author viewed the same film in the company of a number of distinguished Western parapsychologists and some prominent critics of parapsychology. I was unimpressed, as were many of the others in the room. In the film Mikhailova could be seen only from the waist up. Small magnets taped to her knees could easily have accounted for the rotating compass needle or for moving the metal objects about. Other objects might have been moved by kicking the table gently. It is also possible that threads could have been attached to the objects, and these would not have shown up in the film. A halfway competent conjurer could easily have produced the same effects. The individual who had obtained the film said that he presumed that those who tested Mikhailova and made the film checked for this sort of fraud, but he did not know. In their report on Mikhailova's activities, Ostrander and Schroeder are extremely vague concerning the controls under which this sensitive operates.

Despite its shortcomings, the Mikhailova film has become popular among some parapsychologists in the

United States. Dr. Krippner has shown it to several groups and says that he believes that Mikhailova's PK power comes from some sort of electrostatic effect. He claims that he, too, has been able to master the ability to move small objects about and that the ability improves with practice.

Most Western parapsychologists, however, have hesitated to endorse the claims made for Mikhailova and have expressed extreme caution, in some cases bordering on absolute skepticism, regarding the claims made for parapsychology in the Soviet Union. They have also expressed great sympathy for their Eastern European colleagues who often conduct their experiments in the face of official disapproval and hostility. They stress that the techniques of parapsychology in Eastern Europe are still inferior to those of the West and that the Eastern parapsychologists seem doomed to repeat many of the errors that plagued the pioneer parapsychologists of the West.

While machines may one day allow parapsychologists to construct a perfect experiment to test ESP, there is an extremely difficult problem that the machines cannot solve and probably will just make worse. ESP, if it exists at all, appears heavily dependent upon the emotional or psychological state of the subject. Parapsychologists had long suspected that people who believed in the possibility of ESP did better on ESP tests than skeptics. In 1958 this idea itself was tested by Dr. Gertrude Schmeidler. Before putting subjects through a series of standard card-calling tests, she interviewed them regarding their attitudes toward ESP. Those who tended to believe were called affectionately "sheep," while those who tended to disbelieve were labeled less affectionately "goats." The sheep did better than the goats on the test, not much better, but the parapsychologists regarded the difference as significant. Researchers have also found that it helps if those conducting the experiments also believe in ESP. This, they say, is the major reason why skeptical scientists seem unable to get good results when they try to repeat some of the classic ESP tests. The skeptics, however, point to other studies which indicate that those who tend to believe in ESP make recording and other errors, which favors the ESP hypothesis.

If mood and attitude are so important to ESP, it is natural that parapsychologists would be deeply interested in what effect various psychoactive drugs that affect the mind might have on ESP abilities. This interest is not a new one. The great American psychologist, and psychical researcher William James (1842–1910) experimented on himself with peyote and nitrous oxide, better known as laughing gas. In the 1930s Rhine used both sedatives and stimulants on some subjects. The sedatives seemed to reduce scoring, while the stimulants increased it, but the tests were not thorough enough to be considered conclusive.

Throughout the 1950s and early 1960s, individuals who had experimented with psychedelic drugs reported extrasensory experiences. Such stories, while interesting, had little value as scientific evidence.

Attempts to test the effects of drugs on ESP have proved to be extraordinarily frustrating. In the first place, psychadelic drugs like LSD got a very bad name in the U.S. during the 1960s and their legal use was severely limited by the government. It became difficult even for recognized research institutions to obtain the drugs they needed for tests. Worse still, subjects under the influence of psychadelic drugs often refused to cooperate with standard tests.

The Maryland Psychiatric Research Center was one of the few places in the U.S. where research with psychadelic drugs was conducted legally in the 1960s. Some pilot experiments with LSD did not produce encouraging results, for the drug actually seemed to drop scores below chance level. The late Dr. Walter Pahnke, director of clinical sciences at the center, told the 1970 Parapsychology Foundation convention that subjects were often fearful or ill when they took drugs and thus too preoccupied to take ESP tests. "Psychedelic drug effects can also be so novel, dramatic and interesting," he said, "that a subject may have some reluctance to attend to such a mundane task as guessing the content of a sealed envelope."

Still Pahnke was not discouraged. "The possible effect of psychedelic drugs on ESP phenomena provides an exciting challenge for parapsychological research in the future," he said.

Psychic Spectaculars

One of the most well-publicized "psychic events" of recent years took place on September 17, 1967. In a television studio in Toronto, Canada, the Right Reverend James A. Pike, former Episcopal Bishop of California, sat with Arthur Ford, a minister of the Disciples of Christ Church and one of America's best-known trance mediums. They were to hold a televised seance that had been arranged by Allen Spraggett, religion editor of the *Toronto Star* and a frequent writer on psychic subjects.

Ford put on a blindfold—to protect his eyes from the strong TV lights he said—and went into a trance. During the trance Ford's spirit guide "Fletcher" delivered messages allegedly from the spirit of Bishop Pike's son, Jim, Jr., who had shot and killed himself in New York about a year earlier.

According to Ford, Fletcher was the spirit of a long dead French Canadian who regularly transmitted messages from the spirit world.

Aside from the television cameras, the seance with Bishop Pike was very traditional. The "messages" from the "spirit" of James Pike, Jr., were the same sort of consoling, morally uplifting, and rather vague communications that mediums had been delivering in the name of the spirits for over a century.

During the seance the "spirits" of James Pike, Jr., and others who had messages for Pike were supposed to have produced some evidence of their genuineness—that is, they were supposed to have revealed information about their earthly lives that could not have been known to the medium by ordinary means. This evidence, however, turned out to be of a not very high quality, and it was delivered in a rambling, disjointed, and tentative fashion. Some months after the seance I asked Bishop Pike about this information. He admitted that the medium might have obtained it through normal means, from mutual friends or newspaper reports. Bishop Pike stressed, however, that he in no way believed that Arthur Ford had done this and affirmed his conviction that during the seance he had been in contact with the spirit of his son.

Prior to the seance Bishop Pike himself had been no hardened skeptic about psychic subjects. Though a clergyman, he had suffered from many of the religious doubts that had tormented the founders of psychical research during the nineteenth century. His religious views had always been unorthodox, and at the time of the seance he had been charged with heresy and had resigned his position as Episcopal Bishop of California. His interest in psychical research went back several years prior to 1967, and he had written that he hoped psychical research would provide him with the kind of scientific proof he needed to retain a belief in the immortality of the soul.

In yet another way Bishop Pike was very typical of those who are drawn to spiritualist seances. The suicide of his son was a crushing personal loss, and he sought solace through the agency of spirit mediums. Ford was not the first medium he consulted. In the period immediately before and after his son's death, Bishop Pike had spent much of his time in London, where he had allegedly been put in contact with the spirit of Jim, Jr., by the British medium Ena Twigg. Incidentally, Jim, Jr., had also shown some interest in spiritualism while attending school in England shortly before his suicide.

Bishop Pike did not rush to a seance immediately upon learning of his son's death. He was driven to spiritualism after he came to suspect that he had become the focus of poltergeists and other strange manifestations. The Bishop decided that he had to go either to a medium or to a psychiatrist.

Objects, including photographs of Bishop Pike and his son, seemed to disappear mysteriously and then reappear once again in unfamiliar places. Strangest of all was the apparent recurrence of the 140° angle. Bishop Pike found an alarm clock that had belonged to his son had stopped at 8:19. This he believed was the time of the boy's death by London time (Jim had shot himself in New York, and the coroner had estimated the time of death to be 3 A.M.). The hands of a clock set to 8:19 form a 140° angle. Quite suddenly it seemed that the 140° angle appeared everywhere. A batch of opened safety pins that were found mysteriously on the Bishop's bed seemed to form the fatal angle. Books or cards fell on the floor in such a way as to create a 140° angle. According to an article in *The New York Times* on September 19, 1967, the Bishop, after delivering a speech, suddenly "had a great awareness that the hour was important, and almost without thinking," he said, "I turned and looked up at the large clock. 8:19! The configuration of the hands hit me with an almost physical impact . . ."

Milk went sour when it was not supposed to, and Bishop Pike recalled that this had often been attributed to the action of witchcraft or to some other supernatural activity. Was it possible that the spirit of his son was trying to "get through" from "the other side"?

It was this series of experiences that led Bishop Pike first to the parlor of Mrs. Twigg (after some unsuccessful experiments with a Ouija board) and ultimately to the television studio in which he taped his seance with Arthur Ford.

The reaction to the Ford seance was sensational. The tape was first shown on Canadian television and then widely in America. A story of the seance and the events that led up to it appeared on the front page of *The New York Times*, one of the few times in its long history that the influential newspaper has given front page coverage to a psychic event. Naturally other papers and magazines throughout the country picked up the story.

There were plenty of scoffers, of course, and many

prominent parapsychologists were extremely cautious and would not endorse the genuineness of the phenomena. One even suggested that the various poltergeist manifestations might be the result of some sort of mean practical joke being played on the Bishop. All too often in the past a practical joke had lain at the base of a poltergeist case.

These warnings, however, were forgotten by most, and publicity for the case continued to build as Bishop Pike, Arthur Ford, Ena Twigg, and Allen Spraggett appeared on television throughout the U.S., Canada, and England. The Bishop and his wife, the former Diane Kennedy, began a collaboration on a book about life after death. And then the case of Bishop Pike took one final grim and bizarre turn.

In the fall of 1969 Bishop Pike and his wife went to the Holy Land to do research for a book he was planning on the origins of Christianity. On September 1 they left Jerusalem in their rented car, driving in the direction of Bethlehem. It should have been a short, pleasant outing, but the drive took the couple through the area near the Dead Sea, one of the most barren and unfriendly regions on earth. During the trip they took a wrong turn, became lost, and ultimately their car got stuck in a washout. All attempts to free the vehicle proved useless. The couple was now stranded without water or other supplies in the midst of a trackless desert. For two hours they walked trying to find their way in a landscape without any familiar landmarks— for all they knew they had been walking in circles. As night neared, both were exhausted, and they knew that if they did not find help soon they would perish.

Diane Pike, who was considerably younger and stronger than her fifty-six-year-old husband, felt that she had the strength to push on in what she was sure was the direction of the Dead Sea. The Bishop declared that he could go no farther, but urged her to continue and, when she reached safety, send help back for him. Ten hours after they had become lost, Diane Pike stumbled into an Israeli construction camp and the search for Bishop Pike began.

Once again Bishop James A. Pike was front-page news in many parts of the world. The thought of this colorful and controversial clergyman lost in the very region where tradition says Jesus prayed, fasted, and was tempted, held an irresistible fascination for journalists and their readers. But the search for Bishop Pike was more than a physical search conducted by Israeli helicopters and army patrols—it turned into a psychic search as well with mediums and psychics from around the globe joining in.

Two days after the Bishop's disappearance, Mrs. Pike received a message from Arthur Ford, who stated that he had psychically seen Pike alive in a desert cave. Mrs. Twigg phoned from London to say that the missing man "was on the border trying to make the transmission." A medium in Tel Aviv held a pendulum over a map, and by its swinging she marked a spot at which Bishop Pike should be found. She also received, by automatic writing, a message from the spirit of the late

American mystic Edgar Cayce, who said that Pike was still alive but in a coma.

Six days had passed since the breakdown in the desert, and searchers were pessimistic, saying that no one could survive in the waterless Judean desert that long. Diane Pike herself had a vision of her husband's spirit leaving its body, ascending to the sky and being greeted by a great crowd, including his son and Bobby Kennedy.

The following day Israeli searchers found the body of Bishop James A. Pike. It was on a ledge, not in a cave, as Ford's vision had indicated, and it was not at the spot picked by the Israeli medium. The Bishop had been dead for some time and apparently had not survived his desert ordeal for long.

Shortly after Bishop Pike's death Arthur Ford also died. While doing research for a biography on Ford, Allen Spraggett and the Rev. William V. Rauscher turned up evidence that cast a cloud of doubt over his original televised seance with Bishop Pike. In Ford's files they found old newspaper clippings that contained some of the information that had supposedly been revealed by the spirits during the seance.

Spraggett also quoted a former secretary of the medium who said that Ford often had extensive notes about prospective sitters at his seances because nobody could "perform 100 per cent of the time."

Spraggett acknowledged that the discovery was a "traumatic moment," but, according to a March 11, 1973 *New York Times* story, he asserted that Ford was a "gifted psychic who for various reasons, scrutable and inscrutable, fell back on trickery when he felt he had to."

As far as providing evidence either of survival after bodily death or of the psychic abilities of any particular medium or sensitive, the case of Bishop Pike is about on a par with the celebrated ghost and medium cases of the late nineteenth and early twentieth centuries. That is to say, while the case is extremely intriguing, the quality of evidence is not very high. But for most people, what they know about psychic forces or psychical research comes from newspaper, magazine, or book accounts of just this sort of "psychic spectacular." For this reason we are going to examine a few of the more celebrated cases and colorful individuals on the modern psychic scene. We will try to see how well these publicized cases correspond to scientific standards for proof of extrasensory perception. It is vital for anyone truly interested in the subject of ESP to understand that publicity and proof are not the same.

If a sensational crime, particularly a murder, remains unsolved for long, you can be quite sure that a psychic will be asked by private individuals to offer his solution to the case. Generally the police either ignore the intervention of the psychics or are actively hostile toward them. But occasionally the psychics are listened to, and the results can be unhappy ones.

In 1959 the police were stymied in their investigation of the brutal and apparently motiveless slaying of a husband and wife and their two daughters. Friends of the Dutch-born psychic Peter Hurkos induced him to take on the case. Hurkos worked primarily by psychometry or getting psychic impressions from objects. After handling a piece of evidence, Hurkos described the murderer as a man whose business was "either junk or garbage." As it happened, the police already strongly suspected a trash collector but had no solid evidence against him and were reluctant to attempt an arrest. However, fortified by the psychic's reading, they induced the man's wife to sign papers that would commit him to a mental institution. A rushed lunacy hearing was held at 3 A.M., and the unfortunate trash man was adjudged insane and whisked off to an institution two hundred miles from his home. Only prompt action by civil liberties lawyers managed to get the man out of the institution, and doctors there conceded that he was not insane. Somewhat later, the FBI, through the use of conventional investigation methods, arrested another man who was later convicted of the crime.

A number of publications that were prepared to run articles about Hurkos's "success" quietly shelved their plans. Yet the devoted supporters of the psychic refused to concede that he had made a near tragic mistake, or indeed that he had made any mistake at all. One psychic investigator called Hurkos's performance "fantastically successful." The mistake, he contended, had resulted from faulty police work. According to the Hurkos partisans, the psychic had really identified two men, the trash man and the real murderer. What had happened, they said, is that Hurkos had identified the real murderer through psychometry. He had named the trash man through telepathy because the police had already suspected him and Hurkos had read their thoughts. They say he reported his psychic impression in a confused manner, and the police first arrested the individual they had previously suspected. Unfortunately, the only ones who seemed to have known about this second and correct identification were Hurkos's friends. The public became aware of his "fantastic success" only after the second man had actually been arrested.

A few years later Peter Hurkos became involved with an even more noteworthy case, that of the Boston Strangler. In the early 1960s an unknown killer stalked the Boston area, murdering at least eleven women by strangulation. Despite the most intensive investigation in Boston police history, they were unable to identify the killer or stop him. The city was reduced to a state of near panic. Women living alone double-locked their doors and bolted their windows; many purchased huge watch dogs and refused to go out at night. Yet the murders continued. There was a great public outcry to "do something." Into this emotionally charged situation stepped Peter Hurkos. He had been brought to Boston by a group of wealthy admirers who paid his expenses and his fee. The Boston police were suspicious of the psychic and refused to cooperate with him in any way, but another official group investigating the crimes did avail itself of his services.

Hurkos dazzled the investigators with a display of his alleged powers. He related all sorts of personal information, some of it quite embarrassing, about the investigators themselves. They were impressed, but the fact is that all of this information could have been obtained by perfectly normal means. When it came to producing the one piece of information he could not have obtained by ordinary means, the piece of information for which he had been brought to Boston in the first place—the identity of the Boston Strangler— the psychic was far less successful. He came up with an identification all right, but again it was the name of a person whom the police already suspected. Hurkos made the identification after he was given a letter that the man had written. This person turned out to be mentally ill, but quite harmless. The suspect was institutionalized but later released. When the real Boston Strangler finally was identified, he turned out to be a very different sort of person than the one described by Peter Hurkos. The press savagely denounced the official use of the psychic, though some of the papers had earlier helped to publicize his exploits.

Another Dutchman, Gerard Croiset, has also developed a reputation as a "crime solving" psychic. For years Croiset worked closely with Dr. W. H. C. Tenhaeff, formerly director of the Parapsychology Institute of the University of Utrecht in Holland. This association has given Croiset a measure of respectability that most other professional psychics lack since they generally dislike being tested too closely.

Though Croiset has rarely worked in the United States, his name is quite well known, primarily through the efforts of writer Jack Harrison Pollack. A close look at one of Croiset's cases will show why psychic spectaculars are so easily misinterpreted by the general public.

In a 1961 edition of *This Week* magazine, a popular Sunday supplement, Pollack wrote of the success that Croiset had in helping to catch a man who had assaulted a young girl with a hammer in the town of Wierden, Holland. The average reader simply accepts such a story at face value if he is inclined to believe in extrasensory perception at all. He has no way of checking it out. But parapsychology critic Mark Hansel was not the average reader; he did decide to check further. He sent a copy of the *This Week* story to the police of Wierden. He received a reply from the town's burgomaster (mayor), who also served as head of the local police. According to Mark Hansel, the burgomaster expressed astonishment: "How is it possible that a simple story can be mutilated in such a way?" he wrote. According to the burgomaster the story even had the basic facts of the assault wrong. When it came to the explanation of Croiset's "solution" to the case, the burgomaster was downright indignant.

The police, he said, had never called the psychic in on the case. Their only involvement was that one policeman was present when Croiset examined the hammer used in the assault. Croiset could easily have known something of the case before he arrived on the scene. He lived only seventeen miles from Wierden and had once worked there as a delivery boy. The hammer had been on display in the window of a local grocery store in the hopes that someone would be able to identify its owner. Croiset was able to describe the store but could do nothing with the hammer until he was told that it had been used in a case of attempted murder. He then went on to describe, in a rather vague way, a young man with a deformed ear as the guilty party. As it happened, a young man was already under suspicion, and when he was later picked up for another crime, he confessed to the hammer assault as well. He had two normal ears, and about the suspect's age, Hansel says, the burgomaster commented, "Anybody will give young men a greater chance to do such silly things." Thus, in the opinion of the burgomaster of Wierden, who had been on the scene, Croiset not only did not "solve" the crime, as the article had contended, but had, in fact, been no help at all.

Hansel wrote to *This Week,* pointing out the errors in the story, but the magazine did not publish his letter or any other form of correction. As a result the story continued to circulate. It was picked up, errors and all, by a popular Canadian magazine.

Three years after the original article appeared, and after its author had been made aware of Hansel's criticisms, he wrote a book about Croiset. The Wierden hammer story appears once again, and although some of the details had been changed to square with Hansel's criticisms, the book account still gives completely the wrong impression—that Croiset had somehow been instrumental in solving the crime.

The performance of four other "crime-solving psychics" was investigated by Dr. F. Brink, a Dutch police inspector. His conclusion, stated in an article in the *International Criminal Police Review* was: "Several tests were marked by a diversity of procedure and circumstances. Those made during a period of over one year have not evinced anything that might be regarded as being of actual use to police investigation."

Dr. Brink was struck by the fact that the psychics almost always expressed themselves in the form of tentative questions. "May it be possible that————?" If they got an affirmative answer, they would immediately try to create the impression that they had scored a direct hit rather than that they had been merely probing, Dr. Brink asserted. Even when no verbal reaction was given to such probing, there are a variety of involuntary reactions, expressions, movements, etc., that can tip an observant psychic off as to whether he is on the right track or not.

Like the actions of mediums of the past, the activities of the modern crime-solving psychics are open to a wide variety of interpretations. Supporters are convinced that people like Hurkos and Croiset provide proof positive of the existence of psychic powers. Critics like Hansel and Brink are equally convinced that such activities prove nothing except the gullibility of the press and public. As indicated, professional psychics generally resist entering a parapsychology laboratory. They say that stringent laboratory conditions hamper their abilities. Critics contend that such stringent conditions would soon reveal that the psychics possessed no unusual abilities at all.

Gerard Croiset and Dr. W. H. C. Tenhaeff, working at the University of Utrecht, however, have devised a non-laboratory test, called the chair test, that has received a great deal of publicity. Croiset gives a lot of lectures. Occasionally on the morning of the lecture, or the day before, he will take a seating plan of the lecture room, sit down before a tape recorder with Tenhaeff or one of his associates, and predict who will be sitting in a particular chair at the lecture. Not only does he attempt to describe how the occupant of the chair will look on the night of the lecture, but he also gives details of the person's life. Assuming that Croiset does not plant a confederate in the predicted chair, the test seems simple and almost foolproof. After the lecture Tenhaeff or one of his associates will question the subject extensively in private about what Croiset has said. Unfortunately, even in the best of the chair tests, there remains an infuriating vagueness.

One of Croiset's most successful tests, and one that has been cited frequently by Tenhaeff and others as proof of the Dutchman's psychic powers, might be titled "the case of the woman in the white blouse." It took place in 1953, on the day of a lecture that Croiset was to deliver in the small town of Pirmasens, Germany. Croiset recorded that he was going to make a prediction about the person who would be sitting in chair number 73 that evening. Martin Ebon in his book *Prophecy in Our Time* says that Croiset saw the chair being occupied by a lady of about thirty years or younger, who "often wears a vest made of angora wool. But on this night she is wearing a white blouse." There followed a number of more or less personal details, but of a general nature.

There were 250 people at the lecture, more than had been expected, and some additional chairs had to be set up. As a result, the seating in the room was not exactly as it had appeared on the chart that Croiset had looked at earlier. When he entered the room, Croiset told Tenhaeff that the woman he had described was in the room, but not in chair 73; she was now sitting two seats away from it.

Upon seeing the woman and questioning her later, Tenhaeff established the following points. The woman was thirty-two years old and wore a white blouse. As she was about to take this blouse from her closet, she saw a vest of angora wool that she owned and considered whether it might not be wiser to wear the warmer garment that evening.

Croiset had also said he saw the symbol of an "all-seeing eye"—an eye within a triangle. Croiset later interpreted the "all-seeing eye" as a symbol of keen intelligence, and investigators concluded that the woman in the white blouse possessed keen intelligence.

These statements seemed direct hits by Croiset, but some of his other statements were less satisfactory. He mentioned her suffering "an upset" in a delicatessen, and something about a box of dates. The woman said that she worked near a delicatessen, but did not particularly recall anything about a box of dates. Delicatessens are common in Germany.

Most of Croiset's hits could have been the result of coincidence or a generous interpretation of a general or ambiguous statement. The most damaging fact in the face of Croiset and Tenhaeff's claims for the psychic's precognitive powers was that he had failed to actually predict who was to be sitting in chair 73. True, the seating had been rearranged, but if Croiset could see the sort of vest a woman he had never met owned, why was he unable to foresee the change in seating? He could quite easily have walked into the lecture room, looked about for a woman in a white blouse (surely not an uncommon figure at lectures), and then told Tenhaeff that she was the one he had meant, no matter what seat she was sitting in. The only truly impressive hit, therefore, concerns the angora wool vest. But here, too, coincidence might be the answer, for angora wool vests were common articles of clothing.

The most spectacular of all psychic spectaculars—at least the one that seems to make the deepest impression on the public at large—is the prophecy of some important unexpected national or world event.

Professional and semi-professional prophets regularly claim that they had predicted certain events—but the prediction is made public, or explained, only after the predicted event has taken place. There were, for example, many psychics who claimed that they had predicted the assassination of President John F. Kennedy in 1963. One of these prophetesses, Jeane Dixon of Washington, D.C., was made nationally famous by the prediction because she had made it in print eight years before the assassination took place. Actually she didn't really predict the assassination of John F. Kennedy. The prediction appeared in an article written by Washington columnist Jack Anderson for the Sunday supplement *Parade* (May 13, 1956). It read, "As for the 1960 election, Mrs. Dixon thinks it will be dominated by labor and won by a Democrat. But he will be assassinated or die in office 'though not necessarily in his first term.'"

This is something less than a firm prediction of the Kennedy assassination—but it is impressive at first glance. Yet it is a prediction that anyone could have made and that many others did make. It is a bizarre statistical anomaly that every president elected at twenty-year intervals has either been assassinated or died in office. The starting point for the cycle is 1840 when William H. Harrison was elected. He died in office shortly thereafter. Twenty years later Abraham Lincoln was elected, and he was assassinated. James A. Garfield, elected in 1880, twenty years after Lincoln's election, was also assassinated. So was William McKinley, elected in 1900. The next president to die in the cycle was Warren G. Harding, who was elected in 1920 but died in office. Then Franklin D. Roosevelt, elected in 1940, died in office. And of course the cycle continued when John F. Kennedy, elected in 1960, was assassinated.

Only two presidents elected in this twenty-year cycle lived out their terms. They were Thomas Jefferson and James Monroe, both elected before 1840. The only president to die in office who was not elected during the cycle was Zachary Taylor, elected in 1848 and died in 1850.

This cycle of deaths is not quite as astounding as it first appears. Lincoln was elected in 1860 and then reelected in 1864. He was assassinated after his reelection, but he became part of the cycle on the basis of his first election. William McKinley was first elected in 1896 and reelected in 1900. He, too, was assassinated during his second term, but he only became part of the cycle on his reelection. Franklin D. Roosevelt was elected four times. He was first elected in 1932, but does not become part of the cycle until his third term in 1940. He died at the beginning of his fourth term.

As early as Harding's day, prophets of various sorts were warning of the dangers to presidents elected during the "fatal twenty" cycle. Prophets tend to repeat certain themes; therefore, it is hardly surprising that Jeane Dixon, among others, would repeat the warning in her prophecies. She was right in predicting that a Democrat would win the 1960 election (a fifty-fifty chance) but wrong in saying that the election would be dominated by labor. Thus the famous prophecy turns out to be not much of anything at all. Its fame, indeed Mrs. Dixon's fame as a prophetess, comes primarily from the fact that her friend, the syndicated columnist Ruth Montgomery, had regularly printed her predictions.

There are, of course, many other stories concerning Jeane Dixon and the assassination of President Kennedy. Some contend that on the very day of the assassination she had tried desperately to warn him of the danger. But these stories depend almost entirely on the word of the prophetess's friends. Such stories are interesting, often dramatic, but they simply cannot serve as evidence.

Mrs. Dixon's other predictions, by the way, are usually so vague as to be uncheckable, or often turn out to be quite wrong. Yet because of publicity her reputation persists.

If any sort of extrasensory perception exists, proof of it will not be found in well-publicized psychic spectaculars. We must look to the less sensational but infinitely more reliable work of the professional parapsychologists.

7

Strange Abilities

Like all frontier areas of human knowledge, parapsychology, or psychical research, has no hard and fast
borders. The investigation began primarily to test the
hypothesis of survival after bodily death. This proved
to be an extraordinarily difficult task and one that did
not lend itself to laboratory studies. Dr. J. B. Rhine
admitted that after decades in the field of parapsychology, he had never seen or heard of a really adequate
investigation of the survival hypothesis.

Since the early years of psychical research most of
the effort has been aimed at investigating the areas of
telepathy, clairvoyance, precognition, and psychokineses. But those interested in psychic phenomena have
by no means confined their efforts to these areas. They
have been willing to tackle almost anything that seemed
to indicate the existence of powers or forces beyond
those accepted by more orthodox scientists. Some of
these investigations have been conducted on the border-

line of magic and the occult, whereas others would appear to fit more comfortably into physical rather than psychical research. But in order to get a balanced view of the scope of modern psychical research, we will take a brief look at investigations of some strange abilities.

Dowsing

Dowsing, water divining, or water witching is the most widely believed psychical or magical practice in the Western world. Hard-headed country folk who would scorn visiting a spirit medium and even look upon card-guessing tests as "foolishness" will call upon the services of a water dowser with as little embarrassment as city folk when they hire a plumber.

Dowsing is the apparent ability of some individuals to locate water, metal ores, or other valuable substances beneath the surface of the earth by employing some unknown force. Traditionally, the dowser holds a forked stick in his hands and walks back and forth over an area until he reaches a spot where the stick begins to vibrate rapidly. Here the dowser believes is the place where water is closest to the surface and where a well should be dug, where the valuable minerals are to be found, or where treasure is buried.

The practice of dowsing is probably quite ancient, but its history can be traced accurately only as far back as the sixteenth century when miners often used forked sticks to locate metal ores. These early dowsers would begin their search by saying, "In the name of the Father, and of the Son, and of the Holy Ghost I adjure thee, Augusta Carolina [the dowsing rods in the sixteenth century sometimes were given the names of recently baptized infants], that thou tell me, so pure and true as Mary the Virgin was, who bore our Lord Jesus Christ, how many fathoms is it from here to the ore."

For the dowser this elaborate religious invocation served a dual purpose; first it called upon God to aid in the quest, and second it helped to ward off the hostility of the established church, which did not look kindly upon such "magical" practices. More than one dowser found himself accused of the dangerous crime of witchcraft anyway. By the eighteenth century religious persecution of dowsers had disappeared, and dowsing became a fairly acceptable practice.

Though it is no longer considered "respectable" by most educated persons—and those with scientific training generally regard it as a superstition—dowsing is still widely practiced in rural areas where water is hard to find. Picking the proper spot to dig a well can save a landowner thousands of dollars. There is no completely reliable scientific method by which the best spot to dig a well can be determined; as a result, people consider dowsing a superior or at least an acceptable alternative to plain guesswork.

In 1967 it was revealed that some U.S. Marines in Vietnam were using divining rods made from coat hanger wire to find land mines, hidden weapons, and tunnels. Use of the wire divining rods was actually being taught, albeit unofficially, at a Marine training camp in Virginia.

Hickory and ash wood are supposed to make the best dowsing rods—though the exact wood of the stick has varied considerably, depending upon what was available to the dowser. Dowsers have also used a variety of other materials, similar to the coat hangers employed by the Marines, including baling wire, steel files, pliers, and any one of a huge number of specially made dowsing gadgets.

Most dowsers are simple people who do not think much about what they are doing; they merely assert that their technique works. A few are exponents of the theory called "radiaesthesia," which attributes all sorts of mysterious radiations to underground water, minerals, and other substances found by the dowser. The claims of the proponents of radiaesthesia have never been scientifically demonstrated and are so bizarre that they have the reputation of being either fraudulent or crankish. More commonly it is believed that the true power of dowsing must lie with some extrasensory faculty possessed by the dowser.

Obviously, dowsing is the sort of activity that interests psychical researchers. There was no great mystery about what caused the dowsing rod to move. Most dowsers grip the rod tightly and in such a way that small involuntary motions of the hands will cause it to vibrate violently. Psychical researchers are very familiar with this sort of involuntary muscular action. It is exactly the same type of involuntary motion that caused the table to tip at seances or the planchette to move across the face of the Ouija board. But this discovery did not dispose of dowsing. Perhaps the involuntary motion was a reaction to the presence of underground water. The first question was not how did dowsing work, but rather did dowsing work at all?

In the 1920s the British physicist Sir William Barrett and the Society for Psychical Research investigator Theodore Besterman examined a large number of cases in which dowsers seemed to be extraordinarily successful in locating water. With two of their best dowsers they tried some experiments such as locating a coin hidden under a covering of one of forty-five chairs. They obtained results that they considered significant, but other parapsychologists believe that these early experiments did not have satisfactory controls.

In 1949 a group of investigators from the American Society for Psychical Research led by Dr. Gardner Murphy sponsored more elaborate dowsing tests. Twenty-seven dowsers were pitted against two scientists in an attempt to locate underground water under a flat sandy slope in Maine. The slope was chosen because the investigators felt that there were no surface indications of where water might be found at a relatively shallow depth. The dowsers and the scientists marked the spots at which they believed that it was best to dig a well, and their choices were tested by actual boring. The scientists did better than the dowsers, whose choices were deemed no more successful than if they had been made by pure guesswork. In a report published in the *Journal* of the ASPR, the investigators wrote, "Not one of our diviners could for a moment be mistaken for an 'expert.' We saw nothing to challenge the prevailing view that we are dealing with unconscious muscular activity, or what Frederic Myers called 'motor automatism.' "

Other tests have produced either negative or inconclusive results. Most geologists attribute whatever success water dowsers may have to the fact that if one drills deeply enough in most places, water will be found. The true test of the water dowser, they say, is to be able to predict how deep the water is and how much water a well will produce. This few dowsers will attempt.

Another possible natural explanation for the water dowser's apparent power is that most dowsers work on land that they know well. America's most successful dowser, Harry Gross, had spent most of his life as a game warden and was very familiar with landforms that sometimes can betray the presence of underground water. Gross admitted that often his rod dipped at the very spot where he had already decided, by conscious reasoning, water would be found. During the 1920s a Major Pogson was the official water diviner of the British-controlled government of Bombay in India. He was unusually successful at finding water in an area where lack of water was a chronic problem. Major Pogson himself, however, believed that he would not have been successful if he had not worked in familiar surroundings.

Clearly, many dowsers are likely to recognize, even unconsciously, certain telltale signs of where water is to be found. Since they are convinced of the reality of their powers, they will respond to this subtle recognition by an automatic tightening of the muscles of the hands, and this in turn moves the rod. However, since water dowsing is so widely practiced and there is such a wealth of anecdotal evidence attesting to its effectiveness, it is a subject that still interests psychical researchers, though tests like the one conducted in Maine are difficult and expensive to arrange.

Somewhat akin to the divining rods are the pendulums that are used for a variety of purposes. Some water dowsers use them instead of rods. Pendulums have been held over maps in an attempt to locate buried treasure. (You may recall that in the search for Bishop Pike when he was lost in the desert a medium held a pendulum over a map of the desert.) Very often they have been held over the bodies of pregnant women in an attempt to determine the sex of unborn children. A common novelty store item is the "sex indicator," a little metal ball attached to a string. According to the instructions, if the pendulum is held over a girl's hand, it will swing in a circular path; if over a boy's hand, it will swing back and forth.

It is a lot easier to test such items as the "sex indicator" than it is to test the claims of a water dowser. Investigators have almost universally concluded that these devices work by involuntary muscular motions and that no extrasensory powers are involved.

Eyeless vision

In 1808 J. H. Desire Pétètin, a doctor at Lyons, France, published an account of some strange observations that he had made during his years of practice. Among the strangest were several cases of spontaneous catalepsy. The patient seemed to fall into a trance during which he or she remained entirely motionless, both pulse and respiration being almost imperceptible. Sometimes Dr. Pétètin found that he could communicate with patients in such a state, but in a most curious way. They seemed to hear him only if he directed his voice toward their fingertips or the soles of their feet, rather than toward their ears. In addition, some of these subjects seemed able to describe medals, letters, playing cards, and other small objects that had been placed on their stomachs but completely concealed from their eyes.

From time to time since Dr. Pétètin recorded his observations, certain individuals have been found who seemed to possess the ability to see or sense with parts of their body other than the normal sense organs.

A virtual eyeless vision craze began in 1963 with reports from the Soviet Union that a young woman named Rosa Kuleshova could read newspapers with her fingertips while blindfolded. Kuleshova's success inspired a host of Russian imitators and was well publicized in the United States. These stories moved Dr. Richard P. Youtz, a psychology professor at Barnard College in New York, to search for the same ability in America. Dr. Youtz proclaimed himself a skeptic, but an open-minded one. He soon located a Flint, Michigan, housewife, Mrs. Patricia Stanley, who could supposedly identify colors with her fingertips. Dr. Youtz said in an address to the Eastern Psychological Association that "eyeless vision" was a "real phenomenon." A few weeks later *Life* magazine was providing its readers with do-it-yourself "eyeless vision" tests.

Eyeless vision has never been of primary interest to psychical researchers in the West, for it seemed too easy to explain on a purely physical basis. It was theorized that subtle heat differences between different colors or between the printed and nonprinted portions of a piece of paper might be detected by persons with an extraordinary sense of touch. If this was how eyeless vision was accomplished, then it was not strictly extra*sensory* perception, but more nearly extra*sensitive* perception. For this very reason Soviet researchers were most interested in eyeless vision. Here it seemed was at least one type of psychic phenomena that could be explained entirely within a materialistic framework.

As it turned out, even this sort of explanation was unnecessary. When the first photos showing Kuleshova being tested were shown in the United States, this author was struck by the fact that the blindfold she wore was entirely inadequate. It was like the blindfold worn by children during a game of pin the tail on the donkey, and anyone who has ever played that game knows just how easy it is to cheat by looking down one's nose and under the blindfold. James (the Amazing) Randi, a professional magician and escape artist, who examined the Soviet photographs along with the author, declared flatly that the tests were a fraud. He said that it would be childishly simple for Kuleshova to look through or around the blindfold. Magicians, he pointed out, were able to do the same thing with much more elaborate eye coverings. "Scientists are not conjurers; they are very naïve about tricks. I have seen them fooled many times."

A Soviet journalist named Lev Teplov came to the same conclusion. He arranged for controlled tests of Kuleshova and some of her imitators. Those who agreed to take Teplov's tests fared badly. He wrote, "It would be wrong to treat all of these 'phenomena' as sheer deceit. Apparently these cases are related to symptoms of hysteria." Kuleshova herself had been a mental patient for many years.

Dr. Youtz's claims were far less sensational than those coming from the Soviet Union and his tests more carefully controlled. He often had his subject, Mrs. Stanley, attempt to identify different colored chips by handling them inside a light-proof box. But even here the magicians asserted that the tests were far from foolproof and that it would have been possible for Mrs. Stanley to receive sensory clues from the chips themselves, without ever being consciously aware of them. Unfortunately, attempts to test Mrs. Stanley under different and more rigorous conditions proved impossible, for after the initial burst of publicity, she seemed to loose her ability.

As usual, American parapsychologists had been far less enthusiastic about endorsing the early eyeless vision claims coming from the Soviet Union than had many American journalists. In the *Newsletter of the Parapsychology Foundation* in the winter of 1966, they tried to strike a balance: "Parapsychology in the Soviet Union is suffering from some of the growing pains with which parapsychologists in the West are quite familiar. . . . The avalanche of enthusiasm for Rosa Kuleshova represents one extreme of the pendulum; Teplov's denunciations form another extreme. Somewhere in the middle, serious research must continue to progress, steadily, carefully without fanfare or flamboyance."

The case of Rosa Kuleshova has been resurrected once again by Sheila Ostrander and Lynn Schroeder in their popular book *Psychic Discoveries Behind the Iron Curtain.* While they suggest that Kuleshova cheated some of the time, they cite other instances where they believe that cheating was impossible. Unfortunately, most of these instances are second- or third-hand accounts. One is reminded of the reaction of committed spiritualists when one of their favorite mediums is caught red-handed in trickery. Certainly they admit that she is forced to cheat some of the time; after all, psychic powers cannot be turned on and off like a water faucet. However, they assert that there are many other instances where the phenomena produced are "undoubtedly genuine." But such moments seem to come only when no skeptical observer is present.

Psychic photography

During the early 1850s a few professional photographers began producing "spirit photographs." Commonly, these showed a living sitter, and alongside was a shadowy figure, usually identified as the spirit of some dead relative or friend. These early spirit photographs were crude frauds and recognized as such by practically everybody but the spiritualists themselves.

The pictures were easily produced. The photographer took a picture of the living sitter and, while developing it, superimposed a second photo of a dummy or confederate suitably clad in gauze or drapery to give the proper spirit-like appearance. Other spirit photographs were produced by even more obvious means. The photographer would simply superimpose photographs of famous persons who had died on the photographs of a living person. Sometimes a smoky halo was painted around the superimposed photo to make it look more spiritual and to disguise the hard outlines of the cutout. Abraham Lincoln was a favorite subject, and thousands of "spirit photographs" of Lincoln were sold in the years after his assassination.

Other types of spirit photographs were, however, less easy to explain by ordinary means. Occasionally, a photograph would be found to contain strange blobs or blurs, or a faint and ghostly image could be detected. Most of these photos were the result of some sort of defect in the camera or an error in the process of taking the picture. Light leaks were a common source of the strange blobs and blurs, while accidental double exposure could account for the ghostlike images. As cameras and photography have become progressively more sophisticated and foolproof, this type of "spirit photograph" has become less common. Still there exists a small residue of spirit photographs that are regarded as genuine, or at least unexplained by psychical researchers. Spirit photography, however, has never been successfully tested in the laboratory.

In 1967 there was considerable excitement over the photographs produced by an ex-bellhop named Ted Serios. Ted (as he preferred to be called) wasn't doing spirit photography but what was called psychic photography. He would take a Poloroid camera, place it against his head, and snap the shutter. Sometimes when the photo was taken out of the camera, it showed a blurry yet identifiable scene of some distant place.

Ted had been practicing his brand of psychic photography for some years but gained little recognition with it until he came to the attention of Dr. Jule Eisenbud, a Denver, Colorado, psychiatrist with a great interest in psychical research. After examining Ted under a variety of conditions Dr. Eisenbud became convinced of his genuineness and wrote a book called *The World of Ted Serios,* which was published in 1967 with a great deal of fanfare.

Critics immediately asserted that Ted might have produced the photographs by trickery. During the test he often used what he called his "gismo," a hollow tube that ostensibly helped him to focus his "psychic powers" into the camera. The gismo was held between his head and the camera lens. In this gismo the critics contended Ted could have concealed a picture and a tiny light. These would have been sufficient to produce an image on a sheet of film. They also pointed out several ways in which the film could have been fixed before the test took place.

Einsenbud was sure that he had taken adequate precautions against this sort of fraud, and when two reporters from *Popular Photography* magazine showed up in Denver, he welcomed them and invited them to observe Ted in action. The reporters, Charles Reynolds and David Eisendrath, Jr., found Ted an exceptionally difficult subject to observe. In the first place, he did not produce photos on demand. In some sessions nothing resulted, and usually photos were produced only after several hours of trying. In addition, Ted, a self-admitted alcoholic, drank a great deal during these sessions, and his behavior often became unpredictable and even violent.

Reynolds and Eisendrath watched Ted for two days and one night, but nothing happened. On the final day of their stay in Denver, the two reporters thought that they saw Ted try to slip something out of his pocket. When he was challenged, Ted literally threw a fit, and the investigation ended in confusion. Reynolds and Eisendrath wrote a long article for *Popular Photography* in which they contended that Ted's photos could have been produced by trickery and that Dr. Eisenbud's previous tests had been inadequately controlled. The Amazing Randi, the magician, took up the battle and went on television to show how photos very similar to those of Ted Serios could be made by trickery. Reynolds, Eisendrath, and Randi challenged Ted to a test of his powers before a committee of observers under test conditions that they chose.

Dr. Eisenbud hotly denied all the charges and accused Reynolds and Eisendrath of distorting the facts. He asserted that Ted had repeatedly produced pictures under conditions that absolutely ruled out the kind of trickery that they had suggested. Randi's feats, he said, were clumsy approximations of what Ted did, but he would not accept the challenge to test Ted. Instead he issued a counter challenge. He asked his critics to find someone who could duplicate Ted's feats 'in any normal way or combination of ways before any competent jury of scientific investigators."

The acrimonious tone of the controversy would have been quite familiar to any nineteenth- or early twentieth-century psychical researcher who had investigated mediums. During the early years of psychical research, such controversies swirled about most popular mediums. The ending, too, would have been familiar. Neither side picked up the other's challenge, so the question was never resolved. However, little has been heard of Ted Serios since 1967. He has not been tested by any of the established psychical research organizations, who generally stood aside from the quarrel, and today Dr. Eisenbud and his staff seem unwilling to discuss the subject of Ted Serios in public. So while Ted Serios's psychic photography is still occasionally cited as a genuine psychic phenomena, the evidence for this is far from satisfactory.

Currently, the most interesting combination of the

psychic and photography is called Kirlian photography, after its discoverer, a Russian electrician named Semyon Davidovich Kirlian. This type of photography does not use light as a normal camera does. Rather, it employs a high-frequency electrical field that is invisible to the naked eye but will show up on a photographic plate. An object, say a leaf or the human hand, is exposed to the field. Behind the object is a photographic plate. When the plate is developed, the object is often shown surrounded by a multicolored outline or halo that may vary greatly from object to object.

For many years psychics have claimed that all living things are surrounded by an "aura," a sort of halo of colored light that is visible only to those who possess psychic power. Moreover, say the psychics, this aura changes and can give an indication of a person's character, state of health, or emotional condition, and, in fact, Kirlian found during his research that the colors around his subjects did seem to change to reflect internal changes. A Kirlian photograph of a man's hand taken during a period in which the man was highly excited or ill showed colors very different from those surrounding the same man's hand when he was relaxed and healthy.

Do the Kirlian photographs show the elusive aura of the psychics, or are the colors produced by some factor in the process of photography itself? Although Kirlian photography currently has created considerable excitement among many of those interested in psychic phenomena, the process has never really been adequately tested, and for now it would be best simply to reserve judgment.

Healing and stigmatization

Throughout history, in practically every society, there have been those credited with the ability to heal the sick. This apparent power has been explained in many ways. In Christian lands it was assumed that God granted the power to certain individuals to cure disease, but the healer could not work alone. It was also assumed that the patient had to possess sufficient faith in God and in the power of the healer. This sort of "faith healing" is still extremely popular among more emotional Christian groups, but is not considered entirely respectable, or even honest, by the established denominations. There are, however, certain places, such as the well-known grotto at Lourdes in France, where apparently miraculous cures are performed, and some objects, notably the relics of saints, are considered to have miraculous curative powers.

The traditional healer works directly upon the patient, usually by simply placing his hands upon the patient and praying. During the nineteenth century another sort of healer became popular. This was the so-called "medical clairvoyant." He did not cure directly; rather he seemed able psychically to diagnose a person's disease and then recommend treatment for it.

Psychical researchers have long suspected that healers might, in fact, be tapping some sort of unknown psychic power. America's best-known psychic, the late

Edgar Cayce, was also a medical clairvoyant. He would go to sleep or into a trance and diagnose the illness of a person. The person did not even have to be in the room or anywhere nearby, for Cayce claimed to be able to give a "reading" from a scrap of handwriting or a photograph. The treatments that Cayce, and most healers, recommend are generally simple ones drawn from traditional folk medicine.

Cayce and other healers have a collection of testimonials to the success of their cures. A popular healer like England's Harry Edwards may receive thousands of requests every week from persons seeking relief from some sort of affliction, and if some patients are disappointed, a significant percentage feel they have been helped. Edwards himself claims 80 percent of those he treats are helped in some way.

Healing would seem to be a subject almost tailor-made for the investigations of psychical researchers, but, in fact, there has been remarkably little activity by psychical researchers in this area because medical claims are extremely difficult to investigate. Even large medical centers with trained staffs and extensive resources have a great deal of trouble trying to test the effectiveness of a new drug or course of treatment. Such large-scale tests are entirely beyond the resources of parapsychologists who generally operate on a shoestring.

No one denies that there is some sort of link between mind and body in most illnesses. There is an entire medical specialty devoted to psychosomatic (meaning, literally, mind and body) medicine. Some diseases like asthma and ulcers seem to be intimately connected with, if not actually caused by, a patient's mental or emotional condition. Doctors are also very conscious of what is called placebo effect. The placebo is a pill or other substance that is completely without medical value in itself—sugar pills, for example. However, if the patient thinks that the pill is some sort of medicine that will make him feel better, he may actually feel better. In testing new drugs, researchers often divide a test group in half. One-half of the group is given the new drug; the other half receives a placebo that looks like the new drug. Sometimes the placebo works as well or better than the drug. In most of these tests even the doctors who are actually administering the drugs don't know which is the real medicine and which the placebo, for it has been found that the doctor's attitude also has a profound effect upon the way a patient feels and the course of his disease. Some surgical procedures likewise have been found to have a placebo effect. Operations that were once common but later discovered to be ineffective would often make the patient feel better just because he believed that he was supposed to feel better. The power of the placebo is in the patient's belief, his faith, that the treatment will help.

Critics of faith healers and medical clairvoyants say that they are like the placebos and work only because the patients have faith in them, that as individuals the healers possess no special powers. The healers generally counter that they have been able to cure diseases that orthodox medical science has pronounced incurable. The problem here is that no two people respond to illness or treatment in exactly the same way. There are cases where apparently incurable diseases, including cancer, have seemingly cured themselves without the intervention of any healer.

One interesting attempt to test psychic healing powers in the laboratory was undertaken by Rev. Franklin Loehr of the Religious Research Foundation in Los Angeles. A group of forty-eight laboratory mice were all given the same type of wound. One-third of the wounded group was given heat treatments, another third no treatment at all. A final third was touched by a man named Oskar Estebany, a laboratory assistant who seemed to possess some undefinable positive influence on animals. According to a published report, the mice touched by Estebany healed much faster than did the mice in the other two groups. However, there are so many factors, not all of them psychic, that can influence the outcome of a laboratory test of this type. The most obvious one is that the group the researchers hoped would heal faster would almost unconsciously be given better treatment and thus would heal faster, but not because of the touching. Orthodox medical researchers have occasionally been misled as to the effectiveness of a particular treatment for just this reason. The sort of experiment performed by the Religious Research Foundation would have to be extensively followed up on in order to be considered conclusive, and so far it has not.

Akin to healing is the phenomena of stigmatization. This is the name given to the spontaneous bleeding that can occur from the bodies of certain devout persons in imitation of the wounds of the Crucifixion. More generally, the word can be applied to any wound that appears on the body for no known external cause.

The phenomena, though rare, seems real enough. In the 1940s a Belgian stigmatic named Louise Lateau was investigated by the Academy of Medicine in her native land. Her arm was sealed up inside a glass cylinder so that she could not touch it or interfere with it in any way. Spontaneous oozing of blood through the skin of the hand was observed by medical witnesses. A similar effect has been seen when persons under hypnosis have had blisters or welts produced on their skin at the suggestion that they had been burned or beaten.

Is stigmatization, or healing for that matter, an extrasensory or psychic phenomenon? The British psychical researcher D. J. West, in his book *Psychical Research Today*, has speculated, "It may not be too fanciful to suppose that there is a link between these peculiar mind-body effects [stigmatization] and the phenomenon of psychokineses. If thought controls nervous impulses from the brain, as seemingly it must if one believes in free will, and if thought can influence the motion of dice, it is not such a far cry to believe that thought can also effect direct changes in the body. If so, this might also explain certain faith cures in which the progress of organic disease has apparently been influenced by the patient's mental attitude."

This problem remains fascinating, complicated, and unresolved.

Poltergeists

As we mentioned earlier, psychical researchers have interested themselves in poltergeist cases. At first, they simply assumed, as others had for centuries, that a spirit was responsible for the strange sounds, movement of objects, and other inexplicable phenomena some people experienced. But the more they investigated, the less satisfied the researchers became with this simple explanation. One thing that the researchers noted was that the poltergeist phenomena usually centered about a particular person, commonly an isolated, disturbed, or unhappy young person. Quite often they found that the entire poltergeist episode had really been the result of trickery by the young person, who was trying to attract attention or gain sympathy. As a result, some psychical researchers have tended to dismiss the entire field of poltergeist phenomena. Pioneer reseacher Frank Podmore set poltergeists down to the actions of "naughty little girls," though in truth boys were involved in trickery as often as girls.

In recent years, the British investigator D. J. West has been equally tough on poltergeist phenomena. "It is doubtful," he wrote, "if there are any poltergeists in which supernormal physical phenomena really take place. There has scarely been anything approaching a convincing case published by the SPR in the last half century, although scores of poltergeists have been investigated . . . there have been so many examples of excitements by untrained persons, that the soundest-seeming testimony is open to doubt. Until investigators can themselves witness the extraordinary antics of the poltergeist, and can see and photograph the objects while they are actually jumping about of their own accord, the only reasonable attitude is one of severe skepticism."

West's skepticism regarding poltergeist phenomena, however, is not shared by the majority of psychical researchers. Though they admit that trickery and faulty observation are common enough in poltergeist cases, they believe that there are a sufficient number of good cases to conclude that the poltergeist phenomena is a genuine one.

What, in the opinion of these researchers is a poltergeist? Although there is really no consensus of opinion, most theorize in a very general way that the poltergeist is a psychic force that either emanates from, or is released by, the troubled individual who seems to be the center of the phenomena. It is almost as if the emotions of the person trigger uncontrollable psychokinetic activity.

Out-of-the-body experiences

Perhaps you have had the feeling of being "outside" of your own body. I can recall several instances when, while asleep, I felt as if I had floated up to the ceiling and could look down upon my own sleeping form in the bed. At the time, I put this odd experience down to an unusually vivid dream. Some parapsychologists, however, believe that there is more to such a feeling.

In collecting accounts of strange experiences, researchers have found a large number where individuals felt that they traveled outside of their physical bodies. There were reports in which the "traveler" witnessed scenes that were far distant from the place where his physical body lay asleep. A few professional psychics contended that they were able to control this technique. The psychics generally referred to the ability as "astral projection."

As usual, neither the spontaneous experiences nor the claims of the psychics made satisfactory evidence. The possible phenomena of out-of-the-body experiences or OOBEs was particularly interesting to Dr. Charles T. Tart of the University of California at Davis. In 1965 Dr. Tart met a man that he calls Mr. X, who claimed to have experienced hundreds of OOBEs and who was willing to try to produce them under laboratory conditions. The test was conducted in a standard dream laboratory. Dr. Tart hoped that he would be able to detect some sort of physical changes in the sleeping subject during the periods when he felt he was out of his body. Dr. Tart also attempted to test the reality of Mr. X's experience. A piece of cardboard containing a five-digit random number was placed on a high shelf in the equipment room, next to where the subject slept. Mr. X had no ordinary way of knowing what this number was. He was instructed to try to float up near the ceiling of the equipment room, look at the number, and memorize it.

The experiment proved disappointing, for Mr. X had a great deal of trouble sleeping with the electrodes

attached to his head. Only one night of OOBEs was recorded. Dr. Tart says in an article written for the
Winter '67 issue of the *International Journal of Parapsychology* that of this night the technician who moni-
tored the experiment wrote:

"Patient feels he succeeded in the experiment; in the
first [period of] sleep he saw two men and one woman
seated somewhere in the hospital—he pinched them.
In the second [period of sleep] the patient saw me and
he said I had a visitor, which I did. However, it is possible that Mr. X may have heard the visitor cough. . . .
Mr. X states that he patted the visitor on the cheeks
and tried to take his hand but that the visitor avoided
[him]. Mr. X recalls that he left the cot, went under it
and out the door into the recording room and then into
the hallway. . . .the patient did not see the number."

Dr. Tart was unable to confirm the material about
the two men and a woman being pinched. Further-
more, since the test number on the ceiling was not
identified and since he could have learned of the technician's visitor by ordinary means, the results were inconclusive.

Dr. Tart felt that he had somewhat better success
with a second subject, a Miss Z, who was able to report
correctly a five-digit test number after several unsuccessful attempts. Of course, it is always possible that
Miss Z was able to get a peek at the number in a perfectly conventional way.

Dr. Tart's conclusions were modest: " . . . the most
important aspect of the present investigation . . . is not

the tentative findings about Mr. X's and Miss Z's OOBEs; rather the demonstration that OOBEs and similar 'exotic' phenomena are not mysterious happenings beyond the pale of scientific investigation."

What Does It All Mean?

In December of 1969, the influential American Association for the Advancement of Science accepted as an affiliate member the Parapsychological Association, an organization made up primarily of professional researchers. Yet this step did not mean that parapsychology was generally endorsed by a majority of scientists.

Supporters of parapsychology tend to look upon the current popularity of psychical subjects and favorable statements from some respected psychologists as clear evidence that the reality of psi phenomena has been accepted by the scientific world. But, as we said at the very beginning of this book, parapsychology is still a highly controversial subject among scientists. It would be hard even to demonstrate that parapsychology is more scientifically acceptable today than it was nearly a century ago when psychical research first began.

Why has the scientific world's resistance to accepting the reality of psychic phenomena been so stubborn?

Dr. H. J. Eysencyk, a prominent British psychologist and supporter of psychical research, has written in *Sense and Nonsense in Psychology,* "Scientists, especially when they leave the particular field in which they have specialized, are just as ordinary, pig-headed and unreasonable as anybody else, and their unusually high intelligence only make their prejudices all the more dangerous . . . "

Some parapsychologists despair of ever convincing the scientific community of the reality of psi phenomena. Dr. Jule Eisenbud speculated that resistance to psi will never be overcome by lab work or by talking to scientists and intellectuals. Rather resistance will be broken down by the interest of the general public. Certainly the scientific resistance to accepting psychic phenomena remains formidable.

The persistent charge of fraud is one that particularly irks parapsychologists. Every time they have a successful result, they say, critics accuse them of faking. And yet psychical research has certainly been bedeviled by fraud of one sort or another since investigations began. Even more orthodox branches of science, however, have had their share of fraud. The Nobel Prize-winning biochemist James D. Watson said that at least one hoax is discovered in his own field every year.

In practice this means that no psychic experiment— no matter how well controlled it appears to be and no matter how high the reputation of the experimenter— is immune from the suspicion of fraud. The only way to get around this suspicion is to have a repeatable experiment. An experiment that will produce the same results if performed by different scientists is the basic criterion of acceptablilty in many branches of science.

Here is a hypothetical case. A sensitive the quality of Hubert Pearce is discovered by parapsychologist A. He performs at levels significantly above chance on well-controlled tests. But unlike Pearce, or most other high-scoring subjects, his ability does not disappear. He continues to give above-chance scores on tests conducted by scientists B, C, and D, some of whom may have been severe critics of psi phenomena.

An alternative would be to construct an experiment that everybody agreed was foolproof: for example, the VERITAC that had been used by Air Force scientists or Dr. Helmut Schmidt's flashing lights. Then a large number of subjects could be tested, and if even one were found whose scores continually defied chance at significant levels, the charge of fraud could be disposed of once and for all.

But many parapsychologists doubt if such strict criteria will ever be met, at least at our present state of knowledge. Nor do they think such a test is necessary. The strictly repeatable and predictable experiment is valid for the physical sciences, but parapsychology is not a physical science as far as we know. Psychical researchers point out that scientists concerned with the study of human behavior and psychology are unable to construct the sort of predictable and repeatable tests that are standard in physical sciences. Despite this fact, their experimental results are not disputed as sharply as are those of the parapsychologists.

Why then do so many scientists insist on applying tougher standards to ESP tests than to other types of behavioral science tests? Perhaps the answer lies in the attitude expressed by Professor of Psychology at McGill University D. O. Hebb, a leading behaviorist, who, according to Arthur Koestler, frankly declared that he rejected the evidence for telepathy "because the idea does not make sense."

Certainly no scientist worthy of the name can reject facts simply because they conflict with established theories or are otherwise implausible, but the more implausible the theory, the better the supporting evidence must be before it can be accepted. It is far more reasonable for many scientists to believe in trickery, which we all know exists, than in ESP, which seems to violate everything else we know about the universe. In short, as psychiatrist and parapsychologist Gardner Murphy has said in the *Journal* of the ASPR, parapsychology will never become scientifically acceptable "until psi gets a theory that fits."

If ESP were nothing more than a "sixth sense," then parapsychologists might not find themselves, after nearly a century of research, without a theory that fits, indeed without any generally acceptable theory at all.

Six, seven, eight, or more senses can be comfortably fitted into the current framework of scientific thought. Birds, without the aid of maps or compasses, can migrate hundreds or thousands of miles back to the exact spot where they had nested the previous year. Salmon after spending years in the sea somehow manage to return to the same fresh water stream in which they themselves were spawned. Sea turtles find their way across hundreds of miles of open ocean to a tiny island. The exact methods by which these animals accomplish such journeys remain mysterious to us. Perhaps they possess senses that are either absent or very weak in human beings. Certainly, they can do things that human beings cannot do without the aid of mechanical and electrical devices.

Most insects can see the ultraviolet end of the spectrum that is invisible to us. Many fishes seem to respond to magnetic influences. Horseshoe crabs, baby turtles, and a host of other sea creatures are somehow able to crawl directly toward the sea under conditions in which they should not be able to tell where the water is by normal sensory means. Even human beings seem to respond emotionally to atmospheric pressure or the ionization of the atmosphere, neither of which make any conscious impression on us.

This list of "extra" senses could be extended almost indefinitely. The more we discover about the senses of living things, the more varied and wonderful they appear. Therefore, isn't it possible that people, at least some people, can respond to what we call ESP that is ordinarily imperceptible? At first glance telepathy, mind-to-mind communication, appears to be just such a "sixth sense."

We know that the brain produces an electrical charge and that the charge varies with different types of brain activity. These variations show up as wavy lines on the graph paper of the electroencephalograph machine. If the machine can pick up these electrical variations, is it not possible that another brain can also pick them up and somehow convert them into coherent thoughts or pictures, just as a radio picks up radio waves and converts them into intelligible sounds?

The theory is very attractive. When the author Upton Sinclair conducted some telepathy experiments and wrote them up, he called his book *Mental Radio*. But the brain-radio analogy cannot be pushed too far. The electrical activity of the brain is so weak that it cannot be detected more than an inch away from the surface of the head. The only way the EEG can pick up the electrical activity of the brain is through electrodes attached directly to the head. Besides, most physiologists scoff at the idea that the brain contains any structure that seems remotely capable of receiving electrical impulses from another brain and converting them into thought.

The real sticking point, however, is the way that telepathy and other forms of ESP seem to behave. If the transmitting agent for ESP is electricity or some other form of radiation, then it should work best when the "sender" and the "receiver" are close together. In recent years Dr. Karlis Osis has conducted a series of tests which indicate that ESP ability does decline very slightly over great distances. This finding runs counter to the bulk of research, which indicates that ESP works equally well (or poorly) whether the two individuals are in the same room or on different continents. In any event, the decline detected by Dr. Osis is so tiny that it hardly seems to support the belief that any sort of known radiation from the brain can account for telepathy.

Clairvoyance presents an even thornier problem for the sixth-sense hypothesis. Psychical researcher D. J. West writes, "In card tests, the targets do not have to be spread out or presented individually, but can just as well be put close together in a pack and enclosed in an envelope. It is hard to imagine any physical stimuli analogous to light waves and sound waves that would be unaffected by such conditions."

At certain levels modern scientific theory might be more comfortable with psychokinesis. Perhaps Nelya Mikhailova can generate some sort of force of field that can move small objects a few inches beneath her hand. Dr. Stanley Krippner speaks of an "electrostatic effect," though just exactly what this is and how it operates is not at all clear. But assuming there is such a field that can work over short distances, we must still account for the cases in which a bell rings or a picture falls from a wall at the exact moment a person dies a hundred or thousand miles away.

There is worse to come—for all of these difficulties fade to insignificance when we confront the problem of precognition. What sort of radiation or force can come from a target that does not yet exist?

The philosophical implications of precognition are staggering. If there is some way in which the order of a deck of cards can be perceived before the cards are shuffled, then the order the cards will take must also be determined before they are shuffled. Surely this determinism cannot apply only to cards. In Chapter 1 we related the story of a man who "saw" a suicide before it took place. Was the suicide predetermined, too, or to use an older word, was it fated? Is everything from questions of life and death to the order of a deck of cards completely and rigidly determined? If one accepts the evidence for precognition, and the evidence for this form of ESP is every bit as good as it is for any other form of ESP, then the answer would seem to be yes. Unless, of course, our whole conception of time is cockeyed. There have been some attempts to portray time as "flowing" in different directions, but these have not been particularly successful or even understandable.

In recent years some of those who accept the evidence for psychic phenomena have become intrigued by physics. The more physicists have probed the basic structure of matter, the less solid it has turned out to be. By now we all know that matter is composed of atoms and that atoms can be broken up into smaller elementary particles like electrons. But these particles are not really solid; in fact, atoms themselves are not material objects. The world being revealed by basic physics is not a material world—it is a world where waves and particles are one and the same. This sounds like a paradox, and in terms of our ordinary way of thinking it is.

The meaning of these discoveries is not yet understood, even by the physicists who are making them, but they have provided comfort for parapsychologists who are at war with a materialistic conception of the universe. Still this is all negative evidence, and negative evidence of the most ambiguous sort. It in no way indicates how ESP works or, in fact, if ESP is possible.

This, very briefly and sketchily, is what might be called the physical side of the ESP problem. But most parapsychologists, as their self-chosen title indicates, have been more intesested in the psychological or mental side. The world of basic physics is still cold and impersonal, not at all the "friendly universe" for which Frederic Myers had hoped. To many, ESP is not a problem of physics but a problem of "mind," but what is "the mind"? It is a word that is difficult to define. Today the bulk of psychologists would probably say that what we call mental activity is really a direct result of the physical activity of the brain. But parapsychologists and others would disagree. The mind, they say, is something quite beyond the brain.

One of the most popular and compelling theories of ESP holds that there is a "group mind" or "universal consciousness." According to this theory all human consciousness is somehow linked in a vast group mind. The group mind theory was first advanced by parapsychologist Whately Carington about thirty years ago, but it was not really original. Some Oriental religions teach that there is a divine universal totality from which all individuals come and to which they return after death. The psychoanalytic theorist C. G. Jung in his theory of the racial unconscious also came close to the idea of a group mind.

There is, of course, no way at present to confirm such a theory or in any way to link it to what we know about the physical universe. Leaving aside the need for proof, however, how well does the group mind explain ESP? It works pretty well with telepathy. If all minds are connected, then contact with another mind seems reasonable. One obvious problem is how an individual mind can filter out a particular thought or image from the great mass of material in the group mind. Carington was able to propose some interesting though not entirely satisfactory answers to this problem.

The group mind theory, however, begins to get into trouble with clairvoyance. A distant scene might be perceived through the mind of someone else who was observing it; thus, clairvoyance would really be a form of telepathy. What about clairvoyance, however, when the scenes or objects were not being observed by any other mind? For example, what of the subject who can call cards that are laid face down on a table? And when one reaches precognition, the group mind theory simply falls apart, unless one sees a predetermined universe that is accessible to the group mind. The group mind would have to be omnipotent; it would, in short, be another word for God. We would thus all be part of the group mind or children of God. Much parapsychological theorizing has taken this sort of religious turn.

Dr. Gardner Murphy has expanded the group mind idea to include not only the living but also the dead— not that the entire personality of a dead person survives as part of the group mind. He speaks of all mind as being a part of an "interpersonal field." Other parapsychologists speak of the survival of mental fragments or particles, which brings us right back to the problem of survival where the whole field of psychical research began a century ago.

In this theoretical, nonphysical world of interpersonal fields, some parapsychologists see a convergence of the world discovered by modern physicists and the world as intuitively experienced by the great religious mystics of history.

Occasionally, parapsychologists are troubled by the notion that much of what they seem to have discovered may be showing something quite different from what they believed. Perhaps the test results have nothing to do with extrasensory perception, but rather with the nature of mathematics. Sir Aleister Hardy, biologist and past president of the SPR, confessed at a recent parapsychology conference: "I have sometimes been tempted with an awful thought which I hardly dare mention because it is such a terrible thing to admit. . . . It is this: Is it possible that what all these [card guessing] experiments are really demonstrating is a scientific measurement of what we in our ignorance call luck; that some people *are* in fact much luckier, whatever that may really mean, at card *guessing* than others? This, of course, is a shocking thing to be said by a scientist . . . but the point I want to make is that this should in fact be no more shocking to the scientific position today than the alleged demonstration of card-guessing clairvoyance. Each must be held to be *equally* impossible."

At about this time your head may be spinning—I know that mine is. We have gone from relatively simple ideas about "mental radio" to problems of mystic experience, basic physics, and the nature of random numbers. Theorizing at this level is a slippery business, for there is nothing solid to get hold of.

Most parapsychologists do not lean too heavily on theory, for they realize just how weak their position is. They believe that they have demonstrated that there is more to man than a material object operating within distinct physical limitations, just as a machine does. Dr. LeShan said in the Spring 1970 newsletter of the ASPR, "Psychical research has scientifically demonstrated a new concept of man, a new way of looking at others and ourselves, a knowledge that there is more to man than our old concepts allow. And that is the real importance of ESP." What this "more" is neither Dr. LeShan nor anyone else can say with certainty.

Parapsychologists often compare themselves to the physical scientists of the seventeenth century who were discovering things about the world that they could not explain or understand. Some suspect that the phenomena they are exploring may never really be understood, though the effort of trying is worth while. Science writer Arthur Koestler, who discussed the implications of parapsychology in his book *The Roots of Coincidence,* concluded: "The limitations of our biological equipment may condemn us to the role of Peeping

Toms at the keyhole of eternity. But at least let us take the stuffing out of the keyhole, which blocks even our limited view."

Shortly before his death Henry Sidgwick, one of the primary founders of the SPR, told the American psychologist William James that it seemed utterly unbelievable that after twenty years of scientific research and experiment so little progress had been made in unlocking the problems posed by psychical research. Sidgwick said that he found himself in the identical state of doubt as when the SPR was founded.

Many of those interested in parapsychology believe that great advances have been made since Sidgwick's day. Others, including this author, find themselves like Sidgwick in an identical state of doubt. The search remains as frustrating, yet as compelling, as ever.

Glossary of Psychical Research

American Society for Psychical Research, Inc. Reprinted by permission.

AGENT: Person who originates or tries to send an ESP message.

ANECDOTAL MATERIAL: Reports of spontaneous or similar experiences, in narrative form, often undocumented.

AURA: Colors with fluctuating boundaries, alleged by some psychics to surround persons and objects.

AUTOMATIC WRITING: Writing of a person who claims to be permitting his hand to move without his volition.

CALL: Subject's attempt to respond to an ESP target; guess.

CHANCE EXPECTATION: Score which would occur in the long run (if no ESP were in operation), e.g., 5 in a run of 25 ESP cards.

CLAIRVOYANCE: Extrasensory perception of a physical object or event (in contrast to telepathy).

DOWSING: Identifying the location of something concealed, by means of automatism. Classically, the term = locating underground water by the movement of some rigid object, like a hazel wand, held in the hands. Term now also covers attempting to find lost objects, mineral deposits, etc.; and the use of other instruments such as pendulums.

DISPLACEMENT: ESP responses to targets other than those for which the call was intended. *Backward displacement:* ESP responses to targets coming before the intended target. *Forward displacement:* ESP responses to targets coming later than the intended target.

ESP: EXTRASENSORY PERCEPTION: The awareness or reception of information about, or a direct response to, some thought, object or event, when this information or response is not explainable by sensory contact, memory or inference. Subclasses of ESP are *clairvoyance, telepathy, precognition* and perhaps *retrocognition.* (The term "perception" is not to be taken literally, since ESP may be a judgment or feeling, or some other non-perceptual response.)

GOAT: A subject in a parapsychology experiment who states that ESP or PK cannot occur under the experimental conditions (whether or not it can occur under other conditions).

HIT: Accurate response to a target.

OUT-OF-THE-BODY EXPERIENCE: One during which the subject feels his consciousness to be located in a position different from his own body.

PARAPSYCHOLOGY: An area of science dealing with such topics as ESP, PK, or survival after death.

PERCIPIENT: Person experiencing ESP, such as the "receiver" in a telepathy or clairvoyance experiment. The term is sometimes extended to include someone who acts as a receiver in such experiments, whether or not there is evidence of ESP.

PK: PSYCHOKINESIS: A physical change in an object, or in its state of rest or motion, which cannot be explained by ordinary physical processes and is therefore assumed to be due to psi (mind over matter).

POLTERGEIST: (= "*Noisy, rattling spirit*") Disturbances characterized by unexplained physical happenings, such as loud noises, sudden movements and breakage of household objects. Usually of short duration and limited to a small area, such as a house.

PRECOGNITION: Foreknowledge of or response to something that has not yet happened, when this knowledge or response cannot be explained as inference from present knowledge or as typical of present responses.

PSI: Comprehensive term for ESP and PK.

PSYCHIC (noun): A person who is a sensitive or claims to be a medium.

PSYCHIC (adjective): Paranormal.

RANDOMIZATION: Method of making sure that the sequence of targets is thoroughly random, e.g., by using a random-number table; in this method each digit stands for a certain target, and the order of digits determines the order of the targets.

READING: Messages about a person, usually given in a mediumistic session or a psychometry session.

RETROCOGNITION: ESP of past events, when the information cannot be explained by present knowledge, logical inference or habitual modes of response.

RUN: Group of trials, e.g., 25 trials in ESP card test.

SENSORY CUES: Information which can lead to a correct response by normal means, and which would therefore invalidate an ESP investigation. Examples are: *visual cues*, as from a shiny surface, which reflects the target, or from the experimenter's eye movements toward the target; *auditory cues*, such as unconscious whispering, or body stillness as the subject gropes in the correct direction; *tactual cues* as in muscle-reading where a person who knows the target tenses or relaxes as the subject approaches the target.

SENSITIVE: Person who has demonstrated marked ESP ability.

SHEEP: Subject in a parapsychology experiment who states that ESP or PK might occur under the conditions of the experiment (even if it is considered very unlikely, or if the subject states that others might be able to do it but he cannot).

TARGET: Objective or mental event which a subject is asked to call in an ESP experiment or to produce in a PK experiment. The target in an ESP experiment may be a card, a picture, a thought, etc.; in a PK experiment it may be a certain position at which dice are desired to come to rest.

TRIAL: Single attempt to identify target; or single unit in PK test.

Selected Bibliography

Christopher, Milbourne. *ESP, Seers & Psychics*. New York: Thomas Y. Crowell, 1970.

Cohen, Daniel. *In Search of Ghosts*. New York: Dodd, Mead, 1972.

Ebon, Martin. *Phophecy in Our Time*. New York: New American Library, 1968.

———— ed. *Test Your ESP*. New York: World Publishing Co., 1971.

———— ed. *True Experiences in Telepathy*. New York: New American Library, 1967.

Evans-Wentz, Walter Yeeling. *The Fairy Faith in Celtic Countries*. New York: University Books, 1966.

Gauld, Alan. *The Founders of Psychical Research*. New York: Schocken Books, 1968.

Greenhouse, Herbert B. *Premonitions: A Leap into the Future*. New York: Bernard Geis Associates, 1972.

Hansel, C. E. *ESP: A Scientific Evaluation*. New York, Charles Scribner's Sons, 1966.

Johnson, Raynor C. *Psychical Research: Exploring the Supernatural*. New York: Funk & Wagnalls, 1968.

Koestler, Arthur. *The Roots of Coincidence: An Excursion into Parapsychology*. New York: Random House, 1972.

Ostrander, Sheila, and Schroeder, Lynn. *Psychic Discoveries*

Behind the Iron Curtain. Englewood Cliffs, N.J.: Prentice-Hall, 1970.

Podmore, Frank. *Mediums of the Nineteenth Century* (2 vols.). New York: University Books, 1963.

Pratt, J. Gaither. *Parapsychology.* New York: E. P. Dutton, 1964.

Prince, Walter Franklin. *Noted Witnesses for Psychic Occurrences.* New York: University Books, 1963.

Rhine, J. B. *Extra-sensory Perception.* Boston: Bruce Humphries, 1964.

————. *New World of the Mind.* New York: William Morrow, 1971.

————. and Pratt, J. G. *Parapsychology: Frontier Science of the Mind* (rev. ed.). Springfield, Ill.: Charles C. Thomas, 1972.

Rhine, Louisa E. *ESP in Life and Lab.* New York: Macmillan, 1967.

————. *Hidden Channels of the Mind.* New York: Sloane, 1961.

————. *Mind Over Matter.* New York: Macmillan, 1970.

Ryzl, Milan. *Parapsychology: A Scientific Approach.* New York: Hawthorn, 1970.

Schmeidler, Gertrude, ed. *Extrasensory Perception.* New York: Aldine Atherton, 1969.

Sidgwick, Eleanor Mildred, ed. *Phantasms of the Living.* New York: University Books, 1962.

Soal, S. G., and Bateman, F. *Modern Experiments in Telepathy.* London: Faber & Faber, 1954.

Soal, S. G., and Bowden, H. T. *The Mind Readers.* London: Faber & Faber, 1959.

Tyrrell, G. N. M. *Apparitions* (rev. ed.). London: Gerald Duckworth, 1953.

West, D. J. *Psychical Research Today.* London: Gerald Duckworth, 1954.

Index